239.91
Na.Ne

The New Evangelicalism

THE NEW EVANGELICALISM

by
RONALD H. NASH

ZONDERVAN PUBLISHING HOUSE
GRAND RAPIDS, MICHIGAN

Library of Congress Catalog Card No. 63-15740

Printed in the United States of America

to

MY PARENTS

PREFACE

Most writers use a preface to tell their readers what they intend to do. This preface will be different. Chapter 1 of this book sets forth my essential aims and goals. But there remains the task of informing my reader about some of the things I have *not* tried to do. And this is important, for I realize that many may wonder why certain topics that appear (and indeed are) relevant to the subject at hand have been omitted.

For one thing, I have not attempted to relate the new evangelicalism to segments of orthodoxy other than fundamentalism. There are hosts of Reformed, Presbyterian and Lutheran Christians (to mention only a few) who, while maintaining their theological orthodoxy, would still insist on being distinguished from both fundamentalism and evangelicalism. Many may wish that I had related neo-evangelicalism to some of these groups, but I believe that this would have introduced several weaknesses into my effort. First, it would have broadened the scope of this work to such an extent that the "strict focus" I desired would have become blurred. The present theological scene within orthodoxy is exceedingly complicated. My aim has been to view only one aspect of that scene. Furthermore, the contrast between evangelicalism and present tendencies within the Lutheran and Reformed churches is neither as clear-cut nor as important as that separating evangelicalism from fundamentalism. Finally, to have turned my attention to many of these groups would, in some instances, have taken me far afield from the areas with which I am best acquainted. We all belong to a rather narrowly defined religious *milieu* and this writer is no exception. Perhaps others will wish to make just this kind of contribution, i.e., concentrate their attention on the relationship between neo-evangelicalism and, for example, Lutheranism or Calvinism. As I remark in the last chapter, this book presents "only a *partial* picture of *some* of the trends in *one* of several movements within contemporary Christian orthodoxy. Our discussion has been *intentionally* limited in scope."

I did give some thought, however, to including a chapter relating evangelicalism to dispensationalism. One of the main arguments of this book is the claim that the new evangelicalism and fundamentalism do not differ doctrinally. The one exception to this is the fact that whenever and to whatever extent that fundamentalism is characterized by dispensationalism, then it and evangelicalism *do* differ doctrinally. As far as this writer knows, no attempt has ever been made to trace the mutual interdependence between contemporary fundamentalism and dispensationalism. Extensive reading in fundamentalist literature and years of personal contact have convinced me that the two movements are largely (though not perhaps completely) co-extensive. In fact, Clarence Bass (in his book, *Backgrounds to Dispensationalism*) has even argued that many of the peculiarities of contemporary fundamentalism are due to its close association with dispensationalism. We are not claiming that all who might be called fundamentalists are also dispensationalists but, speaking generally, one can see how that over a period of time the two movements have joined hands and in some instances have fused into one. Support for this may be found in the doctrinal statements of several fundamentalist denominations which require an acceptance of some of the basic tenets of dispensationalism. While we thus recognize that a chapter on dispensationalism would have made our argument more complete, we believe that it would necessarily have been a superficial discussion. While this writer is convinced that there is a thorough-going refutation of dispensationalism, he is not naive enough to suppose that he could present it in one chapter. Besides, others have written more ably and with more available space than this book could presently afford. It must suffice here simply to point out that one of the basic disagreements between evangelicalism and fundamentalism is over the matter of dispensationalism.

I also thought that something ought to be written about the attitude of the new evangelicalism toward science. Certainly their different approaches toward the relating of science and religion constitute one of the most marked differences between evangelicalism and fundamentalism. However, it is obvious that the problem is just too big to be included within scope of this present work. To be comprehensive, such a chapter would have to discuss such things as evangelical attempts to formulate a philosophy of science consistent with Christianity, as well as evangelical answers to such complicated problems as the age and origin of man, the extent of the flood, the nature of religious and scientific language, etc. The reader can see that an adequate discussion of these topics would really be the beginning of another book — one which would, in fact, dwarf this work. These topics are too important and too complicated to be given only a cursory treatment. The interested reader will find these issues dealt with in such volumes as the American Scientific Affiliation books, *Modern Science and Christian Faith* (now somewhat out of date) and *Evolution and Christian Thought Today;* in Bernard Ramm's epochal but controversial book, *The Christian View of Science and Scripture;* in Gordon Clark's chapter on "Science" in his *Christian View of Men and Things;* and in other books cited in the bibliography to this work.

RONALD H. NASH

TABLE OF CONTENTS

Part One

EVANGELICALISM AND FUNDAMENTALISM

'The Fundamentalist Renascence'

It has been only a few years now since Arnold Hearn, writing in *The Christian Century*, took notice of what he called "The Fundamentalist Renascence." He reported, "Something has been happening within fundamentalism. Away from the centers of ecclesiastical power and theological education of the major denominations, there has been a remarkable renascence of intellectual activity among fundamentalist scholars."[1]

Hearn was indeed correct when he stated that something was happening within fundamentalism — perhaps more correct than he realized. For this revival of fundamentalist scholarship that Hearn noticed is rapidly becoming a new force to be reckoned with on the theological scene. As Hearn himself remarks, it is time for "non-fundamentalist seminaries to begin giving a new kind of serious attention to the revitalized exposition of that twentieth century American expression of Protestant orthodoxy known as fundamentalism."[2]

What Hearn did not see in 1958 was that this new movement was more than fundamentalism becoming intellectual. It was a movement that would not hesitate, in its defense and presentation of orthodoxy, to criticize even itself. In fact, this "new evangelicalism," as it came to be known, insisted that there were factors that set it apart not only from liberalism and neo-orthodoxy but from fundamentalism as well. Harold John Ockenga, who coined the term, "neo-evangelicalism," explained the new position in this way:

[1]Arnold Hearn, "Fundamentalist Renascence," *Christian Century*, April 30, 1958, p. 528.
[2]*Ibid.*

The new evangelicalism breaks with . . . three movements. The new evangelicalism breaks first with neo-orthodoxy because it (evangelicalism) accepts the authority of the Bible . . . He (the evangelical) breaks with the modernist . . . in reference to his embrace of the full orthodox system of doctrine against that which the modernist has accepted. He breaks with the fundamentalist on the fact that he believes that the Biblical teaching, the Bible doctrine and ethics, must apply to the social scene, that there must be an application of this to society as much as there is an application of it to the individual man.[3]

However, not all of orthodoxy is happy over this "revitalized exposition of fundamentalism." To its friends, evangelicalism is simply and plainly historic Christian orthodoxy speaking to the theological, philosophical and social needs of the twentieth century. To its enemies (and evangelicalism has gathered a large crop of them) it is a dangerous position led by men who are accused of being divisive, of compromising the faith, of appeasing evil, of leaning toward neo-orthodoxy, etc. This book is largely concerned to discover which of these is the true picture of the new evangelicalism.

The aims and purposes of this book are set forth as follows: (1) This book attempts to answer some of the many questions that people are asking about the new evangelicalism. What is it? What conditions or circumstances have brought it about? How and why does it disagree with fundamentalism? What differences exist between it and the so-called neo-orthodoxy of the dialectical theologians? What contributions are the leaders of neo-evangelicalism making to the fields of theology, philosophy and sociology? What are the implications of these contributions? This book cannot hope to answer all of the many questions that need answering. Indeed, there may be no answers, in a complete sense, for a number of years.

(2) This book attempts to clear up some of the many misunderstandings about evangelicalism. So many charges and counter-charges have been made that many half-truths and complete falsehoods are being propagated about this

[3]Harold John Ockenga, "The New Evangelicalism," *The Park Street Spire,* February, 1958, pp. 4, 5.

new movement. An attempt must be made to "clear the air" so that the reader, whatever his theological background, may be better able to evaluate neo-evangelicalism for himself.

(3) This book attempts to answer objections that are being raised against the evangelical approach to such questions as the inspiration and inerrancy of the Bible, ecumenicity, separatism and cooperative evangelism.

(4) In an incidental way, this book will touch on some matters that have been crying for an open discussion. It is our hope and prayer that our presentations of these matters may be of help to those whose questions have previously gone unanswered.

(5) Most important of all, this book will attempt to tell the evangelical side of the story. Neo-evangelicals have written many books, but none that set forth their position as a whole. A number of fundamentalists have exposed all that they think is bad about it. It is now time to see on a large scale what good may be said about evangelicalism.

There will undoubtedly be those who will think that these controversies ought to be ignored. Unfortunately, things have gone too far to ignore them. The Christian Church is not being told the whole truth about neo-evangelicalism. We do not believe that this book will add any fuel *to* the fire. Rather, it is our hope that by clarifying some of the issues we may throw some water *on* the fire.

One of the biggest obstacles that one encounters in an attempt to discuss evangelicalism and fundamentalism is the ambiguity of the terms that one must use. Because of this it seemed advisable to use certain key terms — *orthodoxy, conservativism, fundamentalism,* and *evangelicalism* — with purposely assigned meanings. The procedure of assigning and then consistently using definite names is of utmost importance in an investigation of this kind. It should be remembered, however, that in their ordinary usage these terms carry a great degree of ambiguity with them. For example, many Christians who remain fundamentalists in name are really evangelicals at heart.

I shall use the terms "orthodoxy" and "conservativism"

synonymously as designations of "that branch of Christendom which limits the ground of religious authority to the Bible."[4] At all times, this book recognizes that orthodoxy is broader than either fundamentalism or evangelicalism. There are many orthodox or conservative Christians who would not wish to be considered as either fundamentalists or evangelicals. The views of such people are not in view in this book except insofar as their positions touch on the subject at hand.

The word "fundamentalist" may be used in at least two senses: In the broadest sense of the word, all orthodox Christians are fundamentalists since they believe in what have come to be known as the five fundamentals: the infallibility of God's revelation in the Bible, the virgin birth, vicarious death, bodily resurrection and the second coming of Christ. However, since the word has acquired connotations that go far beyond a mere acceptance of the basic tenets of orthodoxy, we shall not use "fundamentalism" with this meaning. In its narrow sense, "fundamentalism" is used today to refer to the American reaction against religious modernism at the turn of this century that based its defense of orthodoxy on the fundamentals of the faith. Later, we shall notice that one of the major arguments of evangelicalism (in fact, it is almost its *raison d'etre*) is that contemporary fundamentalism has forfeited its right to be considered the historic successor of the early fundamentalists.

The word "evangelical" may also be used in two senses. In its broadest meaning, an evangelical is anyone who believes and preaches the Gospel (in Greek, *euangellos*). To avoid confusion, we shall use the word only in its narrow sense to refer to the advocates of neo-evangelicalism, the recent reaction within orthodoxy to fundamentalism.

Any book of this kind has to be selective. The best way to give a brief picture of any movement is to concentrate on the writings of some of its leaders. The men we have chosen to consider include: Edward John Carnell,

[4]From *The Case for Orthodox Theology* by Edward John Carnell, p. 13. © W. L. Jenkins, 1959. The Westminster Press, Philadelphia. Used by permission.

a professor at Fuller Seminary; Carl F. H. Henry, editor of *Christianity Today;* Bernard Ramm, a professor at California Baptist Theological Seminary; Gordon Clark,[5] director of the department of philosophy at Butler University; and Harold John Ockenga, pastor of Boston's historic Park Street Congregational Church.

The reader should always remember the danger of misrepresentation that exists whenever an entire movement is studied through the writings of a few of its leaders, especially when that movement is as loosely organized and as difficult to particularize about as neo-evangelicalism. We should be content now with knowing what the tendencies are. Only time will fully tell where these tendencies will lead.

[5]This writer has noticed that lately Clark's name has been left out in discussions of neo-evangelicalism. Nevertheless, he was one of its "founding fathers" and still represents its basic position.

CHAPTER 2

From Fundamentalism to Evangelicalism

From Fundamentalism to Evangelicalism

Comparatively little has been written about the conditions and circumstances that brought about the transition from fundamentalism to evangelicalism. We believe that a study of the history of fundamentalism in the twentieth century will reveal four major steps in this transition.

I. FUNDAMENTALISM BEFORE WORLD WAR II

A. *The Fundamentalist Reaction to Religious Modernism*

The rise of religious liberalism and the subsequent reaction of fundamentalism is a story that has been told so often that one can safely assume a general acquaintance with the subject. However, the desirability of making our account complete seems to require some discussion at this time.

During the latter half of the nineteenth century, significant changes took place in many areas of theology. The philosophies of Kant and Hegel had gained many professors of divinity as converts and these converts proceeded with militant and "evangelistic" zeal to adapt the thinking of the entire Christian Church along the lines of their reinterpretation of Christianity. Schleiermacher and Ritschl became the leading standard bearers of this retreat from biblical Christianity. The new theological ideas spread rapidly throughout Europe and began to be felt in America.

However, the impact of German liberalism upon American theology would not have been so great had it not been for other factors. The natural sciences began to earn more respect among the masses as their technological advancements added to man's knowledge and their practical application added to his comfort and convenience. Many educated people began to feel that the Humean and Kantian criticisms of traditional Christianity and the implications of Darwinian evolution had made Christian supernaturalism a relic of a dark and superstitious past. In addition to this, the teachings of the destructive brand of higher criticism with its negative attitude toward the Scriptures helped kindle the fires of cynicism and agnosticism. All these things and more seemed to give added emphasis to the belief that there was no more room in an enlightened world for a supernatural revelation and religion.

Generally speaking, conservative Christians were rather slow in awakening to the dangers of religious modernism, as it came to be called. A few, like James Orr, wrote admirable and scholarly defenses of the historic Christian faith.

Gradually, many centers of theological learning in America capitulated to the presuppositions of liberalism and began to graduate preachers and theologians who were often nothing more than humanists in clerical garb. Conservatives began to realize that many schools and churches were being lost to this rationalized brand of Christianity and began to react to it in defense of orthodoxy.

There was a definite need for a reaction to modernism. Conservatives agreed that whatever modernism was, it certainly was not Christianity. It is also a fact of extreme historic importance that during the early years of the orthodox reaction, the controversy was generally waged on a high intellectual level.

After some years, the issues began to narrow. Conservatives believed that modernists were undermining Christianity of its supernatural, foundational, doctrinal elements. They were convinced that without these fundamental doctrines of the faith, there could be no Christianity. The importance of these fundamental doctrines was further emphasized by the publication of a series of twelve small volumes called The Fundamentals.* This project was begun in 1910 and was financed through the gifts of two wealthy laymen. Furniss comments that —

> The primary importance of the work lay in its doctrinal exposition. In addition to several articles on regeneration, sin and other tenets, the series expatiated on the "Five Points" that were to become the *sine qua non* of fundamentalism: the infallibility of the Bible, Christ's Virgin Birth, his Substitutionary Atonement, Resurrection, and Second Coming. The conservative's creed was now reduced to clear essentials; so significant did the undertaking seem that some attributed the start of the fundamentalist movement to the influence of the volumes.[1]

Today, it is possible to look back and see that many of the criticisms the fundamentalists brought against modernism were sound. Carl Henry records that orthodox scholarship showed —

> The gospel of liberalism was not the gospel of the New Testament. The careful and painstaking work of men like Machen, B. B. Warfield, Geerhardus Vos, and to some extent of E. Y. Mullins made it apparent that whatever liberalism appealed to as its authority, its appeal to primitive Christianity was naive or insincere. Liberalism side-stepped the force of fundamentalist arguments by ridicule; the fundamentalists were said to be reactionary and provincial.[2]

But fundamentalism rapidly lost ground in several areas. The forces of liberalism repeatedly gained control of denominations, influential seminaries and colleges and denominational mission boards. These losses, perhaps more than any other factor, awakened the fundamentalists to the seriousness of their situation and spurred them on to tremendous activity. Unfortunately, the value of their work was not always equal to the effort they expended.

B. The Fundamentalist Reduction of Christianity

Christianity desperately needed some kind of reaction against religious modernism. In its early years, fundamentalism gave promise of being just such a reaction. However,

---

*Reissued in one volume, as *The Fundamentals for Today*, Charles L. Feinberg, editor, 1961. Grand Rapids: Kregel Publications; 657 pp., $5.95.
[1]Norman F. Furniss, *The Fundamentalist Controversy, 1918 - 1931*, New Haven, Yale University Press, 1954, p. 13.
[2]Carl Henry, *Fifty Years of Protestant Theology*, Boston, Wilde and Company (c. 1950), pp. 63, 64.

as the years passed, certain tendencies began to develop within fundamentalism that not only threatened its value as a reaction to liberalism but in some respects endangered the cause of historic Christianity. In the next few pages, we shall notice some of these tendencies. However, it should be remembered that in almost every instance, these conditions could be traced back to the nature of the conflict that fundamentalism was waging.

We have already suggested that the fundamentalist emphasis on certain doctrines was necessary. The fundamentalists were correct in arguing that the modernist could not deny the basic truths of the faith without at the same time destroying Christianity. However, the emphasis on a few major doctrines was sometimes carried too far so that all of Christian doctrine was reduced to a few essentials. Fundamentalists were often guilty, for example, of reducing the Christian message to one of salvation alone.[3] They often neglected or underemphasized the importance of Christian growth after salvation. They were often accused of avoiding social problems by asserting that salvation alone was the answer. While the new birth is a powerful force for the good of society, Christians do need more than it in solving the varied and complex social issues of the day.[4]

Another fundamentalist reduction or simplification of Christianity could be seen in the common tendency of the fundamentalist to think of his religious faith as something separate from his everyday life. Reid, himself a conservative, made this observation several years ago in *The Calvin Forum*.

> Many of them (fundamentalists) seem to regard their religion as something separate from the problems raised by economics, sociology and the natural sciences, except where these fields of study make a direct attack upon Christian

[3]This writer regrets the need for such extreme generalizations and recognizes perfectly well that these indictments may not be brought against all. However, these things have been and still are true of too many fundamentalists.
[4]Some writers, in pointing out the *general* failure of fundamentalism to provide adequate answers to social problems, have overlooked *some* positive contributions by the movement. Examples include the temperance movement, city rescue missions and the work of many mission boards in establishing hospitals.

doctrine. In ordinary life, they deal with their business as though they can be neutral about it, while their Christian faith is kept in a separate compartment . . . Most of them, however, have a dichotomy of thinking which enables them to regard the world and its affairs "neutrally," while in the sphere of religion they follow the traditional Christian lines.[5]

Fundamentalists came to believe that evolution was perhaps the most dangerous enemy they faced. Their distrust of evolution, however, often led to a distrust of science. A large number of conservatives did not share this feeling and found ways of reconciling their faith with science. Many, like James Orr, were confident that they could reconcile Christianity with evolution. While most fundamentalists reacted strongly to what they considered to be threats (made in the names of science and Darwin) against their faith, most scientists considered their arguments irrelevant or invalid.

Not the least of the fundamentalist's blunders was his failure to differentiate between Darwinism and the theory of evolution as it had developed since Darwin. James Orr had even warned conservatives of this in no less a source than *The Fundamentals*. He wrote, "Much of the difficulty on this subject (evolution) has arisen from the unwarrantable confusion or identification of evolution with Darwinism."[6] The subsequent failure of fundamentalism to take account of this fact led eventually to many of the tragic defeats which it later suffered in this area.

While we are discussing evolution, it might be helpful to notice a bit more of Orr's article. It seems noteworthy to this writer that the editors of *The Fundamentals* did not believe that Orr's remarks were out of place for a conservative.[7] Orr wrote,

> While it must be conceded that evolution is not yet *proved*, there seems to be a growing appreciation of the strength of the evidence for the fact of some form of evolutionary

---

[5]W. Stanford Reid, "Modernism - Romanism - Fundamentalism - Calvinism," *Calvin Forum*, December, 1948, p. 88.
[6]James Orr, "Science and Christian Faith," *The Fundamentals*, Chicago, Testimony Publishing House (no date) volume 4, p. 102.
[7]In fact, it is quite revealing to study *The Fundamentals* and notice the difference between the positions taken by many of its contributors and the positions of those who today would call themselves fundamentalists.

origin of the species — that is, of some genetic connection of higher with lower forms. Together with this, at the same time, there is manifest an increasing disposition to limit the scope of evolution and to modify the theory in very essential points — those very points in which an apparent conflict with Scripture arose.[8]

Fundamentalists not only reacted to attacks made against Christianity in the names of science and philosophy, they often reacted against science and philosophy as such. For example, Bernard Ramm speaks of the ignoble tradition in fundamentalism which took and still takes an unwholesome attitude "toward science and has used arguments and procedures not in the better tradition of established scholarship."[9]

Fundamentalism's attitude toward science was typical of its depreciation of scholarship in all fields.[10] Furniss, in his *Fundamentalist Controversy*, is undoubtedly biased in some of his remarks but, unfortunately, such a statement as that which follows is all too true:

> Except for J. Gresham Machen and a few others, the conservatives had no leader with an impressive training. Its champions were men whose principal assets were conviction and zeal, not erudition, and whose followers came primarily from rural and southern regions where academic standards fell far below those existing in other sections of the country . . . . Ignorance, then, was a feature of the movement; it became a badge the orthodox often wore proudly. They believed that faith was God's only demand upon His people and that higher education was of limited value, even a handicap in seeking the Kingdom.[11]

Even a conservative like Reid could admit that there were among fundamentalists "the anti-intellectuals who believe that all education is relatively bad and should be avoided as far as possible."[12]

8*Ibid.*
9Bernard Ramm, *Christian View of Science and Scripture*, Grand Rapids, Eerdmans, 1955, preface.
10To some, this might seem like a contradiction of our earlier statement that "during the early years . . . the controversy was generally waged on a high intellectual level." There, we were describing the early beginnings of the fundamentalist reaction to liberalism. Only gradually did it develop a spirit of anti-intellectualism.
11Furniss, *op. cit.*, pp. 38, 39.
12Reid, *op cit.*, p. 88

Fundamentalism failed to supply an adequate and competent literature for many areas of thought. To be sure, the fundamentalists did produce innumerable volumes of published sermons, devotional literature, missionary themes and polemical works against modernism and evolution. But there was no literature showing the implications of Christian theism for aspects of life other than religion. Even in the field of theology, few great exegetical commentaries or theology books were written. However, Carl Henry has admitted that there are some reasons for this dearth of fundamentalist literature.

First, Henry claims that conservatism was busy concentrating on evangelism and missions while these areas were largely ignored by the modernists. Since much of Protestantism had capitulated to liberalism, the task of presenting the redemptive uniqueness of Christianity was left exclusively to orthodoxy. This meant that conservatives "concentrated on applied theology, while liberals concentrated on secularized theology and applied ingenuity."[13]

Secondly, Henry argues that since it became necessary for conservatives to reveal the great disparity between Christianity and liberalism, the best orthodox scholars did most of their writing in the field of polemics. Thus, the efforts of genuine scholars like J. Gresham Machen and Oswald T. Allis were expended in this direction.

Henry suggests still a third reason for the lack of an adequate fundamentalist literature. It was —

. . . not due exclusively to a sterility of fundamentalist scholarship, as the anti-evangelicals have frequently represented it, but equally much to the fact that scholars who were still partisan to biblical supernaturalism were unwelcome at the universities, colleges, and seminaries in which the newer philosophies had made gains. Evangelical scholarship was driven, in considerable measure, to new interdenominational or to the smaller denominational schools, where the academic demands were too strenuous to permit significant production, while denominational funds were turned to support of academic centers committed to modern theology.[14]

[13]Henry, *Fifty Years, op. cit.*, p. 89f.
[14]*Ibid.*, p. 66

There was one more thing that tended to discredit the fundamentalist movement. *Christian Life* magazine reports that "what started out as a high level discussion degenerated into a cat-and-dog fight. The Virgin Birth ran neck and neck with murder on the front pages of newspapers. Evolution was pitted against the Bible in the Scopes trial of 1925."[15] Carl Henry admits that if any one thing has discredited fundamentalism, it has been its temperament and attitude, and not primarily its theology. Henry is thinking especially of the attitude of rancor and negation often found in representatives of the movement although he is careful to add that such a mood has not been true of all who were considered fundamentalists.

> Historically, fundamentalism was a theological position; only gradually did the movement come to signify a mood and disposition as well. Its early leadership reflected balance and ballast, and less of bombast and battle. Only later did a divisive disposition show itself plunging the evangelical (i.e., fundamentalist) movement into internal conflict.[16]

Because of these many factors we have noticed, fundamentalism has become a term loaded with bad implications. "Fundamentalism began to be a catch-all for the lunatic fringe; Holy Rollers, snake handlers, even Mormon polygamists were calling themselves fundamentalists."[17]

Henry summarizes the disrepute into which the term has fallen when he writes,

> By some fundamentalism is considered a summary term for theological pugnaciousness, ecumenic disruptiveness, cultural unprogressiveness, scientific obliviousness, and/or anti-intellectual inexcusableness. By others, fundamentalism is equated with extreme Dispensationalism, pulpit sensationalism, excessive emotionalism, social withdrawal, and bawdy church music.[18]

[15]"Is Evangelical Theology Changing?", *Christian Life*, March, 1956, p. 16f.
[16]Carl Henry, "Dare We Renew the Controversy?", *Christianity Today*, June 24, 1957, pp. 23f.
[17]*Christian Life, op. cit.*, p. 16.
[18]Carl Henry, "What is This Fundamentalism?", United Evangelical Action, July 15, 1956, p. 303.

All of these factors helped to produce a reaction to these tendencies within fundamentalism — a reaction that has come to be known as "The New Evangelicalism."

II. FUNDAMENTALISM AFTER WORLD WAR II

A. *The Fundamentalist Reconsideration of Itself*

During all the years that fundamentalism was a movement, there was "a solid core behind the garish shell. Even before World War II, that core began to push out."[19] After the war, this "younger generation" began to make itself known in theological circles. Many of these men had studied in such centers of intellectual learning as Harvard and Yale. Hearn writes approvingly,

> A new generation of earnest intellectuals is appearing within the ranks of avowedly fundamentalist groups and educational instructions . . . A strand of irenicism runs through their thought. They are able to view other kinds of theology more objectively and appreciatively than their predecessors did in the 1920's and to deal responsibly with these theologies from the standpoint of their own presuppositions.[20]

These men were not averse to criticizing their own movement for what they considered to be its shortcomings. Carl Henry in his book, *The Uneasy Conscience of Modern Fundamentalism* (1947), chided the movement for its lack of social concern and its inadequate system of ethics. Henry wrote in the preface to this book,

> Those who read with competence will know that the "uneasy conscience" of which I write is not one troubled about the great biblical verities, which I consider the only outlook capable of resolving our problems, but rather one distressed by the frequent failure to apply them effectively to crucial problems confronting the modern mind. It is an application of, not a revolt against, fundamentals of the faith, for which I plead.[21]

In 1946 Gordon Clark bewailed the condition of fundamentalism and its lack of competent scholarship in such areas as philosophy, sociology, science and politics. After

[19]*Christian Life, loc. cit.*
[20]Arnold Hearn, "Fundamentalist Renascence," *The Christian Century*, April 30, 1958, p. 528.
[21]Carl Henry, *The Uneasy Conscience of Modern Fundamentalism*, Grand Rapids, Eerdmans, 1947, preface.

all, it was the problems in these areas that were (and still are) agitating our world and the voice of fundamentalism, charged with the responsibility of giving men the Word of God, was strangely silent on these issues. Clark pleaded for a "contemporary Christian literature that studies all phases of intellectual interest . . . (this is) the great need of our age, for fundamentalists have too long neglected their obligation."[22]

As long as fifteen years ago, evangelicals warned that fundamentalism was failing to provide answers to the complex social and ethical problems facing the world. They pointed out that, "Whereas once the redemptive gospel was a world changing message, now it has narrowed to a world resisting message."[23]

Thus, evangelicals were suggesting that like the young man in the gospel story, it could be said of fundmentalism, "Yet one thing thou lackest." Fundamentalism had sought to defend and preserve God's message from the inroads of modernism and unbelief. But it had neglected and overlooked the need of projecting that message into the social and intellectual life of the country. Evangelicals now wished to perform this task but they wanted it understood that in no way should their work be construed as a departure from the "fundamentals" of the faith.

B. *The Fundamentalist Reconstruction Into Evangelicalism*

Evangelicals like Gordon Clark and Carl Henry were not satisfied with a mere criticism of their movement. They sought to correct the very conditions which they thought were detrimental to the welfare of orthodoxy. However, many fundamentalists misunderstood their efforts, objected, and then resisted the proposed corrections. Evangelicals have subsequently been maligned, misrepresented and misquoted. Many have been branded as modernists by uneducated and ill-mannered fundamentalists who have never taken the time to read their writings in context. Earnest

22Gordon Clark in the preface to Carl Henry's *Remaking the Modern Mind,* Grand Rapids, Eerdmans (c. 1946) p. 13.
23Carl Henry, quoted by Dirk Jellema, "Ethics," *Contemporary Evangelical Thought,* Great Neck, N.Y., Channel Press, 1957, p. 133.

attempts to show the implications of the gospel message for
social, economic and political problems are castigated as
returns to the social gospel. All of this has brought about
a growing disparity between what was fundamentalism and
what is now evangelicalism. Some of these differences will
be noted in later chapters.

Hearn finds that the writings of the evangelicals —

> . . . reveal thought which has a comprehensive theological
> concern, is abreast of developments in philosophy and the-
> ology, endeavors to deal honestly with the findings of natural
> science, manifests an interest in social ethics and is striving
> to attain a more than moralistic approach to literature and
> the arts.[24]

Christian Life magazine, in an article entitled, "Is Evangelical Theology Changing?", found at least eight trends in
evangelicalism. These include: a friendly attitude toward
science; a willingness to re-examine beliefs concerning the
work of the Holy Spirit; a more tolerant attitude toward
varying views on eschatology; a shift away from so-called
dispensationalism; an increased emphasis on scholarship;
a more definite recognition of social responsibility; a re-
opening of the subject of biblical inspiration; and a growing
willingness on the part of evangelicals to converse with
liberal and dialectical theologians.

Perhaps the most serious disagreement between fundamentalists and evangelicals is to be found in their respective
attitudes toward non-conservative theologians. Carl Henry
has remarked,

> The recrudescence of fundamentalism during the Second
> World War involved a diversification within the movement.
> On the one side were those eager to detach the great the-
> ological affirmations from a recent negative reactionary
> spirit and to strengthen constructive theological and eccles-
> iastical activity (this would be evangelicalism); on the other,
> those who add to reactionary spirit by multiplying divisions
> and by disowning brethren in the former category (this
> would be fundamentalism). The first group insists that the
> fundamentalists of the latter definition are severing them-
> selves from the spirit of historic evangelical Christianity;

24Hearn, *op, cit.*, p. 529.

the second group claims that the evangelicals of the former category are making a subtle retreat to a compromised fundamentalism.[25]

We have seen how fundamentalism, beginning as a reaction to religious modernism, showed great promise in its early days. However, serious weaknesses soon developed which threatened to obscure the meaning of and hinder the effectiveness of its most important message, the Gospel of Christ. Contemporary evangelicals are seeking to drop the comparatively recent accretions of fundamentalism and return to what fundamentalism was in the beginning.

Christian Life is quite insistent that evangelicalism is taking a positive approach to matters which contemporary fundamentalism is tackling negatively. It writes, "Fundamentalism is still a protest against the mishmash liberal Protestantism made of Christianity. It's still as concerned over preserving the Christian essentials as were the early fundamentalists. But it is something more: a positive witness for God's redemptive love, wisdom and power as revealed in Jesus Christ. In short, fundamentalism has become *Evangelicalism*."[26]

[25]Henry, "Dare We Renew the Controversy?", *op. cit.* (my notes).
[26]*Christian Life, op. cit.*, p. 17

Part Two

EVANGELICALISM AND THE BIBLE

Introduction to Part Two:

EVANGELICALISM AND THE BIBLE

One of the allegations one often hears today is
that neo-evangelicalism has made concessions to neo-
orthodoxy, especially in the areas related to inspiration and revelation. In an attempt to show that this
is not so, we shall in the next three chapters examine
the important subject of the evangelical's attitude
toward the Bible. The problems to be discussed are:
The Inspiration, the Authority and the Inerrancy of
the Scriptures.

The Inspiration of the Scriptures

Whether it be for good or ill, evangelicals are willing to reopen the subject of the inspiration of the Scriptures. Many fundamentalists have misunderstood the reasons behind this and are acting as if they think a "re-examination" of Biblical inspiration means the same thing as a surrender of the doctrine.

The renewed interest in this doctrine is due to the rise of neo-orthodoxy. The emphasis given to the matter of the Word of God by such dialectical theologians as Barth and Brunner together with their criticisms of both the fundamentalist and liberal positions have had a two-fold effect. First of all, theological thought outside of the orthodox tradition has gained a new respect for revelation and the Word of God. Secondly, however, one can notice some loss of confidence in the orthodox view of Scripture in some conservative circles. Thus, the real reason behind this restudy of inspiration is a desire to restate the conservative position so as to contrast it with the neo-orthodox approach. Fundamentalists should try to understand that evangelicals still believe in the "infallibility" and "inspiration" of the Bible, but, as *Christian Life* magazine has put it, they are seeking to define more clearly what these words mean. In 1956, *Christian Life* reported that although this issue, then, might be just a "pebble in the pond of conservative theology, it could expand to be the bombshell of mid-century evangelicalism." [1]

In the rest of this chapter we shall notice some of the main aspects of evangelical thought as they pertain to the problem of inspiration. In subsequent chapters, we shall

[1]*Christian Life, op. cit.,* p. 18.

turn our attention to the subjects of the authority and inerrancy of the Bible.

I. THE EVANGELICAL AND NEO-ORTHODOX VIEWS OF INSPIRATION CONTRASTED

Evangelicalism is firmly committed to a belief in the divine inspiration of the Scriptures. Carl Henry tells us,

> The Bible is no mere record of revelation, but is itself revelation. Revelation is inscripturated . . . This identification of written sentences and propositions with special divine revelation . . . evangelical Christianity hold to be not merely the historic Christian view, but an indispensable element in a proper biblical theology.[2]

With regard to the basic issues involved in relating the Bible and God's revelation, evangelicalism and neo-orthodoxy are at opposite poles of the theological world. Whereas evangelicalism insists that a significant revelation from God must be expressed in words and propositions, neo-orthodoxy repudiates any notion of propositional revelation. Whereas neo-orthodoxy maintains, to put it rather crudely, that the Bible only "contains" the Word of God (that is, the Bible witnesses to but is not itself God's revelation), evangelicalism makes it clear that the Bible, in a fundamental sense, still "is" the Word of God.

Kenneth Kantzer of Wheaton College has summarized a number of the similarities and disagreements between the evangelical and neo-orthodox positions on inspiration. First of all, Kantzer reminds us, "The ultimate object of all Biblical revelation is God as a person."[3] We must remember that the Bible was not given to serve as a textbook on Christian doctrine or as a basis for our church creeds. The purpose of the Scriptures is to bring man into an encounter with the Living God. Simply because neo-orthodoxy has also emphasized this truth is no reason for orthodoxy to de-emphasize it. When orthodoxy ceases to believe and preach this, it will have ceased to be orthodox.

2Carl Henry, "Divine Revelation and the Bible," *Inspiration and Interpretation,* ed. by John Walvoord, Grand Rapids, Eerdmans, (c. 1957) p. 256.
3Kenneth Kantzer, "The Authority of the Bible," *The Word for This Century,* ed. by Merrill C. Tenney, New York, Oxford University Press, 1960, p. 34.

Secondly, Kantzer suggests that the Biblical revelation is concerned to a great extent with divine *acts,* that is, what God has *done* for sinful man.

Thirdly, Kantzer contrasts the evangelical position with the neo-orthodox by pointing out that while the Biblical revelation is personal, it is *also* propositional. This marks one point on which orthodoxy must protest against the dialectical theology. God's revelation is, to be sure, personal; that is, God reveals Himself. But this does not preclude the possibility nor the fact that God also reveals truth about Himself. More will be said about this later.

Finally, Kantzer suggests, "Revelation must be subjectively appropriated."[4] What he means, of course, is that the Bible must be believed and obeyed. The objective Word of God must always be complemented by the internal and subjective work of the Holy Spirit. Thus,

> The cliche, "The Bible *becomes* the Word of God" . . . has a significant element of truth in it. The biblical message came from God whether men receive it as such or whether they do not, but now and again the Spirit of God takes the words of the Bible and makes them subjectively the Word of God to individual men. Instead of the dead letter of the law, the Bible thereby becomes the living voice of the Spirit in the hearts of men. It becomes God's contemporary message, spanning in an instant the millenia between the prophet of old and the men of today.[5]

It is not enough, then, that the truths of the Gospel are only apprehended by man's intellect. The individual must also give his assent to these truths and commit himself to them.

II. COMMON MISUNDERSTANDINGS ABOUT THE ORTHODOX VIEW OF INSPIRATION

Evangelicalism has taken care to point out a number of confusions about and misrepresentations of the orthodox concept of inspiration.

A. *The Mode of Inspiration Was Not Dictation*

Sometimes the evangelical gets the impression that non-conservative theologians have formed a conspiracy to

4*Ibid.,* p. 39.
5*Ibid.,* pp. 40, 41.

caricaturize and castigate the orthodox doctrine of inspiration as a theory of mechanical dictation. This is indeed a
harsh indictment to bring against them, but how else can
one explain their stubborn refusals to treat the orthodox
doctrine for what it really is? Gordon Clark even goes so
far as to suggest, "When the doctrine of verbal inspiration
is so constantly misrepresented, one is tempted to suppose
that the unbelievers found it easier to ridicule dictation
than to understand and discuss verbal inspiration as it is
actually taught by Reformed theologians." [6] It takes a long
stretch of a biased imagination to make any evangelical
theologian teach mechanical dictation. Vernon Grounds
repudiates the charge by writing,

> Subscription to . . . doctrine of verbal inspiration does not
> mean that we think Scripture was produced by a process of
> dictation in which God cancelled out the personalities of
> the writers He worked with and through, using them merely
> as stenographic puppets . . . Scripture was produced by
> the concursive operation of each human author and the
> divine Author — a psychological mystery, to be sure — an
> interaction and inter-relationship in which the human author
> freely exercised every faculty and expressed himself in his
> own distinctive style and vocabulary according to his own
> distinctive intellectual, emotional, and spiritual traits, ac-
> quired from his own distinctive background of heredity
> and experience.[7]

Even though earlier generations of conservative theologians may have used the word, "dictation," it is clear that
they were concerned not so much with the *mode* of inspiration as with the *reliability* or accuracy of the finished product, the Bible.

B. The Result of Inspiration Is Not Bibliolatry

Emil Brunner has accused orthodoxy of making "The
Bible an idol and me its slave." [8] But Brunner obviously
misunderstands the evangelical position. No evangelical

---

[6]Gordon Clark, *Religion, Reason and Revelation,* Philadelphia, Presbyterian
and Reformed, 1961, p. 117.
[7]Vernon Grounds, *The Old Biblicism and the New,* (unpublished paper),
Denver, Colorado, Conservative Baptist Seminary, pp. 3, 4.
[8]From *Revelation and Reason* by Emil Brunner, p. 181. Tr. Olive Wyon.
© 1946 W. L. Jenkins. The Westminster Press, Philadelphia. Used by
permission.

worships the Bible. In no sense at all does it become, for him, a "paper pope." Bernard Ramm has repeatedly tried to bring this to the attention of non-conservative theologians. Writing in the *Christian Century*, he said,

> The authority of Scripture is a delegated one; therefore we must never be guilty of bibliolatry. The supreme content of Scripture is Jesus Christ . . . And therefore the main weight of the word of authority is Christological and re-demptive (and not abstractly juridicial). The written Word of God is sealed to the heart (via the gospel) by the Holy Spirit and therefore it is an authority received with joy . . . and not received (as often alleged) as if it were an auto-cratic and sacrosanct paper pope.[9]

There is, of course, a sense in which the Bible can be regarded as an *end* in itself. It *is* God's written Word to man. But the Bible is and must be seen to be more than an end. In a much more important sense, it is an instrument that we use. It is a *means* to the end of bringing men to the Living Word, Christ.

C. The Corollary of Inspiration Is Not Belief in Inerrant Versions

Orthodoxy limits inspiration to the autographs or the original manuscripts. It clearly recognizes the obvious fact that our present versions contain some errors due to the intricate problems of translating and transmitting the Scrip-tures from language to language, from culture to culture and from century to century.

However, even this notion of an inspired original evokes the ridicule of some. For example, Emil Brunner scoffs at the idea of what he calls the "Bible-X" of orthodoxy. He writes that we can only know two things about this original Bible: "First, that it was the infallible word of God; and secondly, although it was very different from the present one, yet it was still the same Bible." [10] More confusion on this point is evidenced by William Hordern in *The Case for a New Reformation Theology*. He argues, "It is significant that conservatism has retreated (sic) to the point where it

[9]Bernard Ramm, "Authority and Scripture: II," *Christian Century*, March 1, 1961, p. 266.
[10]Brunner, *op. cit.*, pp. 273, 274.

admits that no manuscript of the Bible that we now possess is inerrant." [11] Hordern's misleading generalization implies that orthodox scholars have recently ceased to insist that manuscripts now in existence are inerrant. On the contrary, this writer is perfectly familiar with the conservative literature on this subject and has found it consistently limiting inspiration and inerrancy to the original manuscripts. Thus, it becomes exceedingly difficult to understand how orthodoxy's present position can be construed as a "retreat." We will return to a fuller discussion of this later. It is sufficient, for now, to recall the words of Carl Henry to the effect that even though it is true that no one has ever seen these "infallible originals," it is just as true that no one has ever seen any "fallible originals." Henry's point is that the belief in an inerrant original is as much of an assumption as the belief in a fallible original. Both assumptions are the result of prior theological commitments on the part of theologians and can be substantiated or refuted only on the basis of an examination of these theological and philosophical presuppositions.

D. The Scope of Inspiration Is Not Limited to the Bible

Orthodoxy does not restrict or limit inspiration to the Bible. Evangelicals have been quick to point out that revelation and the Bible are not synonymous. In fact, no generation of Christians has ever equated them exactly. Orthodoxy clearly distinguishes between the written word and the Living Word, a distinction, by the way, that is not always too clear in the writings of neo-orthodoxy. Evangelicals admit that, at times, special revelation has not been written. For example, the exact content of God's visions to Abraham was special revelation but is not recorded for us in the Bible. Thus, revelation is wider than the Bible. However, evangelicalism does take its stand that the Bible is the written form of special divine revelation, that is, in the Bible, God's revelation is inscripturated.

[11]From *The Case for a New Reformation Theology* by William Hordern, p. 58. © W. L. Jenkins, 1959. The Westminster Press, Philadelphia. Used by permission.

III. THE CONTROVERSY OVER VERBAL INSPIRATION

Some fundamentalist critics of evangelicalism are suggesting that evangelicals have surrendered the doctrine of verbal inspiration for a type of conceptual revelation. This is not, by any means, an accurate analysis of the situation.

In agreement with James Orr, I take conceptual revelation to mean, "The theory that revelation and inspiration have regard only to thoughts and ideas, while the language in which these ideas are clothed is left to the *unaided* faculties of the sacred penman." [12] The key to this definition is found in the words, "unaided faculties." A conceptual theory of inspiration would hold that God inspired the ideas alone without any regard for the words in which they are expressed. But such a view of inspiration is not only theologically but also philosophically unsound. In the words of Orr, "Thought of necessity takes shape and is expressed in words. If there is inspiration at all, it must penetrate words as well as thought, must mould the expression, and make the language employed the living medium of the idea to be conveyed." [13]

I understand recent evangelical discussions in this field as follows: evangelicals have simply become more aware of the intrinsic relation that exists between ideas (or concepts) and the words which express them. The famous "Wheaton Statement" on inspiration is an example of this:

> Scripture conveys the thought which God wished to communicate and the thoughts symbolized by these words are all true . . . The biblical writers made their own choice of words, expressed themselves in their own style, and revealed their own particular personalities . . . The message which the biblical writers proclaimed was decidedly their own. God, however, prepared them, illuminated them and divinely energized them, so that their prophetic message would be at the same time His divine message to men.[14]

The statement insists that God "prepared," "illuminated" and "energized" the Biblical writers. Since it is clear, then, that the Wheaton Statement does not leave the expression of

[12]James Orr, *Inspiration and Revelation,* Grand Rapids, Eerdmans, 1952, p. 209 (italics mine).
[13]*Ibid.*
[14]"The Wheaton Statement," *Eternity,* December, 1956, pp. 36ff.

the revelation up to the "unaided faculties of the sacred pen-man," it does not teach conceptual revelation as that theory is usually understood.

Vernon Grounds has given us an even more explicit explanation of the evangelical position. He asks,

Did the Holy Spirit guide the authors of the Bible in the free choice of the words which the vocabulary of each embraced? He did. But He did so in order to convey ideas; and the ideas are the essential factors in the divine revelation with the words, concursively selected by the divine Author and the human authors, functioning merely as vehicles of those ideas. Consequently, in our zeal for verbal inspiration we must not forget that a word in any specific context is the symbol of an idea, the medium of a thought or concept. And for that reason we must not divorce what God has joined together. Undeniably the words are of crucial importance just because of the ideas which they state, ideas which could be stated as God desired them stated by precisely the Word selected.[15]

Dr. Carlton Gregory of Barrington College once suggested the following analysis to this writer: (1) ideas or concepts are necessary to revelation. Without them, there can be no revelation. (2) Words are necessary to the most meaningful expression or communication of abstract ideas, that is, without words the most meaningful communication cannot take place. (3) Any particular word is sufficient to the expression of the desired idea in the original text.

We suggest then that none of the above mentioned statements by evangelicals (which are typical of the evangelical approach to verbal inspiration) should be construed as concessions to conceptual revelation.

IV. CONCLUSION

It ought to be evident to the reader by now that the evangelical position on inspiration is wholly within the orthodox tradition. Many significant issues separate evangelicalism from both liberalism and neo-orthodoxy. If evangelicalism has modified, in any way, the fundamentalist view of inspiration, the modification is a step in the right direction. By that I mean it is a positive step in the direction of a more understandable and defensible position on the inspiration of the Bible.

15Grounds, op. cit., p. 6.

CHAPTER 4

The Authority of the Scriptures

The Authority of the Scriptures

Jesus was once asked the following question: "Tell us, by what authority doest thou these things? or who is he that gave thee this authority?" This same question is asked, in different contexts, hundreds of times each day. All men live under authority of one kind or another. We all recognize the authority of a doctor, a learned professor, a policeman, etc.

One of the most thorny problems in contemporary theology is the question of religious authority. Just as it is only natural and right that we demand to know the authority who bids us act in a certain way or believe in a certain thing, so we should carefully investigate the claims made by a religious body to see if its assertions and dogmas are genuinely authoritative. Because of the crucial importance of religious matters, we owe it to ourselves to see whether our religious authority is, in truth, the authority of God or merely the heavily disguised voice of man. It is of special importance, then, to notice any contributions made by evangelicals in supporting or explaining the authority of Scripture.

Our plan is to notice, first of all, the evangelical criticism of the neo-orthodox view of religious authority. These criticisms, however, should not be viewed as either complete or thorough. Our primary purpose in mentioning them is to suggest the far reaching differences between evangelicalism and neo-orthodoxy. Because of the need for brevity, we have selected Emil Brunner as one whose views are sufficiently representative to speak for many on at least this issue. Then we shall examine the position of Bernard Ramm whose book, *The Pattern of Authority*, is perhaps the major evangelical contribution to this subject within the last few years.

I. Emil Brunner's Concept of Biblical Authority

Paul K. Jewett gives us an insight into the importance of religious authority for neo-orthodoxy. He writes,

> Neo-orthodoxy, like the Reformation and like Liberalism, was born of controversy over biblical authority. In his first German publication, Barth, as a young pastor, trained in German Liberalism, lamented that the modern man no longer acknowledges any authority outside himself . . . Barth was joined by Brunner and an increasing host of lesser known theologians who called the church back to a biblical theology, a theology resting on the authority of divine revelation.[1]

Because of this many have hoped that in Brunner and the rest of the neo-orthodox camp we will find an adequate view of religious and biblical authority. Brunner agrees with the Augustinian principle that God is the final authority in religion and that He expresses that authority through divine revelation. So far, orthodoxy and Brunner are agreed. However, when we investigate Brunner's view of revelation more closely, we shall find a "great gulf fixed" between him and evangelicalism.

A. Brunner's Doctrine of Revelation

Brunner summarizes the heart of his argument as follows:

> Divine revelation is not a book or a doctrine; The Revelation is God Himself in His self-manifestation within history. Revelation is something that *happens*, the living history of God in his dealings with the human race.[2]

The important thing to notice about Brunner's doctrine is his claim that revelation is always and only an event. It is God's breaking into history, into time, in the person of His Son, Jesus Christ. Revelation is not some doctrine *about* Jesus. It *is* Jesus Himself! Since revelation is God's coming to man, Brunner thinks that this therefore makes revelation objective since it comes to man from a source of himself.

---

[1]Paul K. Jewett, "Biblical Authority, A Crucial Issue in Protestantism," *United Evangelical Action*, May 1, 1953, p. 3.
[2]From *Revelation and Reason* by Emil Brunner, p. 8. Tr. Olive Wyon. © 1946, W. L. Jenkins. The Westminster Press, Philadelphia. Used by permission.

As we shall see later, evangelicals have questioned whether there really is an objective element in Brunner's understanding of revelation.

Brunner goes on to tell us that revelation is more than a self manifestation on the part of God. It is personal correspondence. It is an address and a response in faith as the individual is confronted by God in Christ. It is an "I-Thou" relationship. Instead of it being a one-sided affair, revelation is an "encounter" between two persons: God, in the person of Christ, and the sinner. Revelation is an event which is transcendent, unique, absolute, personal and not repeatable. It cannot be proven since it has its own logic and rationality. Christianity cannot be verified by scientific evidence. That which verifies it is simply the uniqueness and transforming inwardness of the experience of faith.

In the encounter between God and man, there is no revealed truth. Brunner and neo-orthodoxy insist that revelation "is not the communication of intellectual knowledge of a doctrine about God, but God's own personal Word ... "[3] And yet Brunner still holds that all sound doctrine is based on divine revelation and is true. Revelation is the basis, norm and criterion of doctrine.

B. *The Delegation of Authority*

(1) Authority was delegated to the apostles and prophets. The reason why human doctrine can spring from divine revelation is due to the fact that in revelation God speaks. Brunner teaches that when revelation occurred in the Old Testament, there was a complete equating of the human word with the Word of God. However, in the New Testament we have a different story, for here we are confronted with a Person, Jesus Christ who is the Living Word. Thereafter, the spoken word is indirect revelation and then, only when it bears witness to the revelation which is Christ. Man's duty is no longer merely to hear the Word but to come, that is, to respond in faith.

[3]From *The Mediator* by Emil Brunner, p. 237. Tr. Olive Wyon. © 1947 W. L. Jenkins. The Westminster Press, Philadelphia. Used by permission.

Brunner states his case as follows: the Church is —

founded upon the "foundation of the apostles and prophets," who point beyond themselves to a revelation which has taken place, and is still taking place, whose witnesses and heralds they are . . . The prophetic word . . . has absolute authority and power. This authority does not reside in the prophet as a person; he himself is "no one"; he is anonymous . . . The prophet has no authority but his "word" has power precisely because it is not his word, but the Word of God, which invests it with divine authority.[4]

The early Church was based upon the oral word of the apostles (Acts 2:42). Eventually, it became necessary to put this oral word into writing and this writing became the New Testament of the Bible.

(2) Authority is delegated to the Bible. Brunner is quite clear about his attitude toward Scripture. "It is clear," he writes, "that the doctrine of the verbal inspiration of the Holy Scripture, which claims to be a standard doctrine, cannot be regarded as an adequate formulation of the authority of the Bible."[5]

But Brunner's argument here is as invalid as it is confused, for it is evident that by verbal inspiration he understands a mechanical kind of dictation. We have already suggested that this identification is unjustified. If conservatives have always used the term, "verbal inspiration," to mean dictation, then Brunner might be correct. But this writer is convinced that evangelicals have not equated the two.

A little later Brunner claims that since the early tradition of historical facts (i.e., the facts found in the Gospels, Acts and Epistles) was "guided and inspired by the Holy Spirit, but was also a product of human research and selection . . . . therefore, it is not verbally inspired."[6] Once again we find that Brunner has mistakenly identified verbal inspiration with dictation so that we are forced to conclude that this argument against verbal inspiration is invalid.

Forgetting for the moment his failure to refute verbal

[4]Brunner, *Revelation and Reason, op. cit.,* pp. 3, 103.
[5]*Ibid.,* p. 128.
[6]*Loc. cit.*

inspiration, Brunner goes on to tell us that the Bible is a human, fallible book. He accepts with open arms the destructive brand of biblical criticism. Since this is so, we are justified in asking Brunner just what authority the Bible does have.

Brunner distinguishes between the spheres of ordinary history *(geschichte)* and salvation-history *(heilsgeschechte)*. The Bible is authoritative only in the latter. The Bible becomes the Word of God in every place where it witnesses to Christ. The doctrines of Scripture are only trustworthy to the extent that they bear this same witness. Brunner asserts, "the Scriptures have the authority of a norm and the basis for this principle is this: The Scriptures possess this authority because they are the primary witness to the revelation of God in Christ."[7]

Since the apostolic witnesses are the only way that the real norm (Christ) witnesses to us, there is an "absolute" sense in which we are bound to this *means*, the medium of the apostolic witnesses, as our religious authority. But in another sense, we are only bound relatively to the authority of this witness, for the Bible is not a *formal* authority, only an *instrumental* one. Thus, the Bible is authoritative only as the *means* and not as the *ground* of the Christian faith.

C. Evangelical Criticisms of Brunner's Doctrine

While it is hardly possible to list all that evangelicals have written in criticism of Brunner's doctrine of religious authority, we believe it is important, in the light of recent fundamentalist claims that evangelicals are compromising the orthodox view of the Bible, to suggest a few of the criticisms they have made. We do not suppose that our brief remarks constitute a final refutation of Brunner's position. Rather, we offer them in the hope that they shall help make it clear that there are many significant differences between neo-orthodoxy and evangelicalism.

(1) Paul K. Jewett has complained that Brunner's

[7]Emil Brunner, *Dogmatics, I, The Christian Doctrine of God,* London, Lutterworth Press (1949) p. 45.

inadequate view of the Bible gives him an inadequate view of religious authority. As Jewett puts it,

> To be precise, Brunner insists that without an authoritative Bible, Christianity is lost (and as a Christian Brunner professedly bows before that authority), but at the same time he tells us that its authority is *conditional*, that it is only an authority freighted with human frailty. Is it not difficult to fit the pieces of this puzzle together?[8]

Since a conditional authority is one that we can talk back to, we can either take it or leave it. It would surely seem then that, to use Brunner's own phrase, "Christianity *is* lost."

Along these same lines, E. J. Carnell levels his cannons at Brunner's concept of salvation-history. Carnell points out that the Bible gives no hint at all of there being any difference between salvation-history and history. In fact, the Bible claims inspiration in both spheres. He asks, "If we cannot trust the Bible's account of itself, how can we trust its account of salvation-history?"[9] Carnell reminds us of the neo-orthodox assertion that it doesn't matter if the Bible blunders about history, for it is still God's valid salvation-history. Carnell's final shot is a telling one. He asks, "If Christ blundered on the data of simple-history, how can he suddenly become an authority when he switches to salvation-history?[10] If Brunner should attempt to avoid the force of his objection by claiming that Jesus was simply accommodating Himself to the false and misleading traditions of His day, Carnell could then justly ask how Jesus could possess even the *moral qualities* (let alone the knowledge) to be our Saviour.

(2) The subjectivism of Brunner's view of revelation makes divine authority equivocal. It is true that Brunner attempts to deny this charge by insisting that there is a difference between subjectivity and subjectivism. He recog-

---

[8]Paul K. Jewett, "Emil Brunner and the Bible," *Christianity Today*, January, 21, 1957, p. 9.
[9]Edward John Carnell, "The Problem of Religious Authority," *His*, February, 1950, p. 8. Reprinted by permission from *His*, student magazine of Inter-Varsity Christian Fellowship.
[10]*Ibid.*

nizes that subjectivism leads ultimately to mysticism and relativism so he claims that revelation is objective since it comes to man from God.

However, Bromily, seeing the dangers implicit in this aspect of Brunner's thought, argues that the neo-orthodox press too far their belief that the Bible is only inspired as the Holy Spirit illumines the individual ego.

> It means that the Bible can be authoritative, not as an outward law, but as the Bible in the individual ego, as an inward experience, and with all Barth's (this goes for Brunner as well) insistence upon the fact that Christianity rests upon unique historical events, with all his stress upon the transcendence of God, in the last analysis we are still left with a faith which depends upon a subjective experience and with the substantial autonomy of the individual ego.[11]

Carnell's main objection to false theories of religious authority is their bad epistemology. He criticizes the religious liberal because he can allow no way to determine between a valid and invalid religious feeling. And since he cannot test for error in his system, he cannot verify its truth. The religious modernist can never be sure that the claims he makes to truth are not merely other instances of the basic error which his methods cannot detect.

Carnell carries this same objection over into his battle with neo-orthodoxy. He shows that the essence of religion for the dialectical theologian is the subjective experience of the crisis encounter. Because of this, neo-orthodoxy is simply an extension of the bad epistemology of religious liberalism, that is, it is a feeling-theology which cannot be validated. Carnell writes, "The trouble with Neo-orthodoxy is, once again, that it cannot test for error. It can no more recognize a valid crisis experience than the modernist can recognize a valid religious experience."[12] Carnell asks, for example, how we can know that tomorrow the witness of the encounter may not tell us that there is no historical second Adam? After all, the neo-orthodox has already asserted

[11]W. Bromily, "The Authority of the Bible: The Attitude of Modern Theologians," *Evangelical Quarterly*, Vol. 19, 1947, p. 135. p. 96.
[12]Carnell, *op. cit.*, p. 8.

on the basis of the same witness that there is no historical first Adam. Brunner might counter by claiming that we know by appealing to the witness of the Christian community as a whole. But Carnell could parry this thrust by pointing out that truth cannot be determined by counting noses. "Perhaps what was dialectically valid yesterday will be dialectically invalid tomorrow. We can only wait and see."[13]

A recent attempt has been made to avoid the force of this objection in William Hordern's book, *The Case for a New Reformation Theology.* We shall examine his argument in an appendix to this chapter. However, until we have looked in more detail at Hordern's effort to rescue neo-orthodoxy, it seems safe to conclude that a view of revelation (such as Brunner's) that makes God's authority equivocal, cannot be adequate.

(3) Bernard Ramm has suggested, "A divine revelation which cannot be significantly called *true* cannot properly express the authority of God."[14] Brunner claims that there are no communicated truths or divine facts in revelation. For him, revelation is simply a personal meeting or encounter. John Newton Thomas has questioned how the Bible can witness to a revelation which it cannot even partially express in language. He has warned that "the status of the Bible is in some respects more precarious than it was before the theologians of the Word appeared on the scene."[15] Thomas believes that this element of Brunner's theology empties the Bible of all inspired truth and he argues that the self-disclosure of God must have a communicable element, i.e., revelation must disclose truth about God.

D. Conclusion

While our above remarks have been brief, we believe that they nonetheless point to some of the major difficulties

[13]*Loc. cit.*
[14]Bernard Ramm, *The Pattern of Authority,* Grand Rapids, Eerdmans, 1957, p. 96.
[15]John Newton Thomas, "The Authority of the Bible," *Theology Today,* Vol. III, No. 2, July, 1946, p. 163.

that any neo-orthodox view of religious authority must face. Let us now see how the evangelical proposes to skirt these problems.

II. BERNARD RAMM'S FORMULATION OF RELIGIOUS AUTHORITY

Bernard Ramm's book, *The Pattern of Authority,* is a fairly recent and systematic attempt to deal with the problem of the Bible's authority from an evangelical point of view.[16]

A. *Ramm's Principle of Authority*

After a brief introduction, in which he discusses authority in general, Ramm poses the basic question: "Is there anything in religion which demands that a man think a certain way about religion and not another? Is there a man, a society, a principle, or a document which has the right to prescribe religious belief?"[17] Ramm wants us to be careful lest we be foolish and reject any truth from God or lest we tragically mistake the voice of man for the voice of God.

Ramm first sets out to find the central principle of authority and then the pattern or ways in which this basic authority expresses itself. He makes it plain that we must "steer a wise course between subjectivism and authoritarianism."[18] It is not enough to say that God is the final authority in religion for we must know how God expresses His authority. Ramm agrees with Augustine that revelation and authority are correlates, that is, God expresses His authority by and through divine self-revelation. He, therefore, arrives at his central thesis, that "in Christianity, the authority-principle is the Triune-God in self-revelation."[19]

[16]We should perhaps point out that not all orthodox theologians are satisfied with Ramm's position. Cornelius Van Til, for example, has objected to Ramm's appeal to Calvin in support of his position. We believe, however, that we can ignore this dispute, for we are only concerned here with the evangelical's attitude toward religious authority and Ramm's position is sufficiently representative of this attitude to enable us to concentrate on him.
[17]Bernard Ramm, *The Pattern of Authority,* Grand Rapids, Eerdmans, 1957, p. 16.
[18]*Ibid.,* p. 18.
[19]*Ibid.,* p. 21.

Ramm shows that there are several advantages and merits to this principle: it avoids both subjectivism and authoritarianism; it avoids the problem which results from trying to find an exclusively written authority since there was no written authority from Adam to Moses and since, in the early days of the church, there was no written New Testament (Acts 2:42); it avoids the danger of substituting the voice of man for the voice of God, as Roman Catholicism does; and finally, it is a personal authority. We believe that even Brunner (so far, at least) would be happy with the merits afforded by this principle.

B. *The Delegation of Authority*

But how is this authority of God delegated? Ramm shows from the history of revelation how revelation came first to certain key persons (e.g., prophets, apostles, etc.) and then was communicated from them to the larger group (either the family, nation or church, as the case may have been). God did not speak His divine Word to every believer but rather to special persons and, then, through them to all believers. The prophet did not have authority because of his person but only because he spoke the revealed Word. "The actual authority for the Old Testament believer was the Holy Spirit speaking the revealed Word through the prophet."[20] Even though the authority was delegated to human and fallible men, there was no diluting of its authority. These men did not possess authority as private persons but only as they spoke and later committed to writing, the revelation of God.

Ramm then goes on to set forth three basic theses: (1) God expressed His authority through revelation; (2) through the ministry of the Holy Spirit, He delegated this authority to chosen men; and (3) through Spirit-inspired men who spoke and wrote the Word, God gave the divinely revealed and authoritative Word to the world. On the basis of these three theses, Ramm then presents what he believes to be the Protestant principle of authority: "The Holy Spirit speaking in the Scriptures, which are the product of the

20*Ibid.*, p. 27.

Spirit's revelatory and inspiring action, is the principle of authority for the Christian Church."[21] It is a dualistic principle which is clearly defined by Bromily when he writes, "We . . . . seek the authority of the Bible in the *balanced* relationship of a perfect form (the objective Word) and a perfect content (the Word applied subjectively by the Holy Ghost) — the form holding the content, the content not applied except in and through the form."[22]

The heart of Ramm's argument is, then, that the principle of religious authority for the Christian is an *objective* divine revelation *with* (and not apart from) the internal, *subjective* divine witness. We suggest that no charge of "biblicism" can be brought against this principle. Ramm insists that he is not advocating some new position. He is merely restating what many of the Reformers (especially Calvin) and many orthodox theologians have been saying for centuries.

In the remainder of his book, Ramm proceeds to trace the delegation of authority further as it applies to the Scriptures, to Christ, to the Apostles, the New Testament and the part that the history of theology plays in religious authority. But as profitable as such a journey would be, to follow the rest of his argument now would far exceed the limits of this chapter.

Needless to say, evangelicalism (by relating the subjective aspect of revelation to an objectively inspired Bible) provides a view of religious authority markedly different from and manifestly superior to that of neo-orthodoxy. It does not leave us at the mercies of subjectivism, relativism and the ever present danger of mysticism (as we find in many forms of "feeling theology"), nor does it force us to bow at the shrine of a "paper pope."

Appendix to Chapter 4

HORDERN ON THE TESTING OF REVELATION

An important part of our argument in Chapter 4 rested on the claim that neo-orthodoxy cannot test for false reve-

[21]*Ibid.*, p. 28.
[22]Bromily, *op. cit.*, p. 136 (italics mine).

lations and thus cannot verify a true revelation from God. A recent attempt has been made to avoid the force of this objection by William Hordern in his book, *The Case for a New Reformation Theology.* Since a lengthy examination and evaluation of Hordern's argument would have introduced a rather long interruption into our discussion of Chapter 4, it seemed best to postpone our consideration of his remarks until now.

Hordern agrees that the matter of verification is an important problem. He argues that there *is* a criterion or standard by which man can judge revelation, but the problem is that this standard can only be given by revelation itself. Hordern rejects the thesis that there are or can be any rational or empirical tests that are adequate and reliable enough to test revelation. His reason for saying this is that God is unique, transcendent and omnipotent. God can be known only as He reveals Himself. Thus, any knowledge of God must be aposteriori. We cannot and dare not set up any a priori criteria and then demand that God measure up to these standards. Only revelation can provide the criteria by which revelation may be judged. He argues, "To make it a condition of God's revelation that he must meet any a priori categories that we set up is to refuse to accept God as God."[1]

This seems like a strong argument. But let us follow Hordern further to see exactly how revelation does verify itself; how he proposes to test for false revelations; and finally, to see if Hordern is perfectly consistent in his argument.

I. How Does Revelation Verify Itself?

Hordern's answer is, "When the Christian confesses faith that Christ is God incarnate, he can only answer 'Why?' by saying, 'Because Jesus is Jesus.' The total impact that he makes upon us is such that we can only respond to him in faith."[2]

---

[1]William Hordern, *The Case for a New Reformation Theology,* Philadelphia, Westminster Press (c. 1959) pp. 81, 82.
[2]*Ibid.,* p. 85.

The reader must notice the implications of Hordern's remarks very carefully. He seems to be telling us that the verification of a religious belief (in this case, faith in the deity of Christ) depends upon the intensity of the subjective religious experience. Such evidence as the testimony of the gospels as to Christ's sinless life, miracles, or teachings are irrelevant or unimportant in the light of one's inward religious experience.

Unfortunately, this entire argument ignores what we take to be the relation of faith and reason in our everyday lives. As an example, let us suppose that someone whom I know to be an habitual practical joker rushes up to me shouting that my house is on fire. Chances are that I would not get very excited for my reason would tell me that the word of this man cannot be trusted. But suppose, instead, that a trusted friend (who is also noted for his sobriety and piety) should rush up shouting that my house is in flames. Would I now respond? I think so! In our ordinary experience, then, an inward response is not excited by what our reason considers to be an irrational report. Edward John Carnell has stated this well:

> In no case (in our daily lives) do we act passionately in defiance of the report of reason . . . The native person — the one unaffected by corrupting philosophic presuppositions — is at his best, and is most ideally a man of faith, when he obeys, rather than defies, the report of a critically developed understanding.[3]

Carnell goes on to add that it is clear that "in our daily living we *proportion* our inward response to the certainty of the evidences . . . . Thus a faith based on rational evidence is able to nourish a healthy inwardness."[4]

Perhaps Hordern might even agree with Carnell's remarks about the relation of faith and reason in daily living but he would undoubtedly add (following Kierkegaard) that this relationship must be suspended when one's eternal happiness is at stake. Kierkegaard has told us that whenever time and eternity meet, the result is always a

---

[3]Edward John Carnell, *Philosophy of the Christian Religion*, Grand Rapids, Eerdmans, 1954, pp. 474f.
[4]*Ibid.*

paradox. However, I believe that a careful analysis of this claim will show that it is wrong. To quote Carnell again,

> If there is any realm where we should expect to rally all our faculties for one harmonious thrust toward truth, it is at the point where our eternal happiness is at stake . . . *The obligation of the will to clear with the verdict of the understanding rises in direct ratio to the importance of the value at stake.*[5]

For example, I might find myself day-dreaming while staring at some passing clouds. I might imagine that one cloud is a chariot and that another is an ancient Greek general. But I can blithely believe *against* the dictates of my reason simply because there are no important values at stake. As Carnell suggests, "The more a value increases, the more our concern should respect the report of reason."[6]

Apparently when a Mahayana Buddhist confesses that Gautama is the incarnation of The Buddha (or God) and Hordern asks, "Why?", the only answer the Buddhist need give is that "Gautama is Gautama!" If the Buddhist's subjective religious experience is intense enough[7], Hordern would apparently have to be satisfied that the Buddhist's religious claim had been verified. Therefore, it seems obvious that to base the verification of a revelational claim upon a subjective religious experience alone leads ultimately to religious skepticism and relativism.

II. How Can Neo-orthodoxy Test for False Revelations?

Evangelicalism maintains that Brunner, Hordern and the rest of neo-orthodoxy cannot test a valid existential experience from an invalid one. There is no way to credit the true religious experience because there is no way to discredit the false. How can we know that it is God we are experiencing and not merely an emotional disturbance

[5]*Ibid.*, p. 477.
[6]*Ibid.*, p. 478.
[7]Or (should Hordern object to my describing religious experience in terms of "intensity") at least exhibit characteristics similar to Hordern's religious experience of the deity of Christ. Any counter-claim that such a similarity of religious experience is impossible would not only miss the point but be most difficult to prove.

or perhaps the devil himself? Since we insist on testing for truth in all other realms, why should we suddenly stop looking for rational evidence when we need it most, namely, when we are seeking to verify a proposed revelation?

Hordern attempts to come to grips with this serious difficulty. Unfortunately, the problem seems too slippery for him. He refers to Soren Kierkegaard's refutation of a heretical minister in his day:

> Kierkegaard found that Adler contradicted his own claim to revelation. Some days Adler insisted that he had a direct revelation; some days he backed down and confessed that it was not really revelation. Adler himself provided the criteria by which Adler was refuted.[8]

This is, indeed, an unfortunate example, for it only reveals how hard-pressed neo-orthodoxy is to avoid this problem. It is sufficient to point out here that if Hordern really means what he seems to be saying, then he would apparently have nothing to say to a consistent spiritist, i.e., one who *consistently* maintained that his "revelation" was true!

III. Is HORDERN CONSISTENT?

Hordern has accused orthodoxy of a priori thinking, i.e., of setting up arbitrary, a priori criteria which it expects God to meet. But, ignoring for the moment whether or not Hordern's complaint is justified (later we shall examine a similar claim by Cornelius Van Til), we must wonder if Hordern himself has been altogether successful in avoiding a priori thinking. A case in point is this paragraph from *The Case for a New Reformation Theology*.

> Despite the fact that we see no possibility of a criterion apart from revelation by which revelation may be judged, this does not leave us at the mercy of the first fanatic to come along. We have every right to test, by reason (sic), any claim to revelation in terms of its correlation with its own claim. As an actual matter of fact, this presents us with the sufficient argument against most fraudulent claims to revelation.[9]

[8]Hordern, *op. cit.*, p. 86.
[9]*Ibid.*, p. 87.

We have been told to expect paradoxes in religion but this does not excuse such apparent inconsistencies in the writings of the theologians of paradox. Under a cover of words, Hordern has smuggled in the law of contradiction and something akin to the coherence theory of truth. Thus, Hordern's proposed testing of the correlation of a supposed revelation with its own claims is nothing more than the application of an a priori test for truth. What Hordern has done, of course, is admit in practice (while denying it in theory) that revelation must not be divorced from reason.

Several leading evangelical theologians have suggested that neo-orthodoxy will eventually take one of two possible avenues: it will turn either to mysticism or to a kind of religious skepticism. If this should ever happen, it need not be the result of any outside influences. It will merely mean that neo-orthodox theologians have finally removed their logical blinders and have followed the implications of their position to its inevitable conclusion.

CHAPTER 5

The Inerrancy of the Scriptures

The Inerrancy of the Scriptures

Much has been written and said about the evangelical attitude toward the doctrine of biblical inerrancy. Hearn reflects something of the common confusion over this matter when he insists that the evangelicals "have not wavered on the doctrine of biblical inerrancy" and then adds that "they sometimes appear to redefine it."[1]

An example of the way in which evangelicals are "redefining" inerrancy is found in an article by E. F. Harrison in *Christianity Today*.[2] Harrison states that there are criteria that conservatives may have once required for biblical inerrancy that today's evangelicals consider excessive and unnecessary. These include such criteria as the insistence that multiple accounts of the same event should use the same words in describing it; the insistence that all statements of Scripture at all periods should be complete and final (Harrison holds instead that there is a progress of revelation and response to the Word of God); the insistence that quotations be verbally exact (he points out that the biblical writers often quoted from memory); the insistence that any difficulties should be judged as errors; the insistence that biblical statements about natural phenomena be scientifically accurate (Harrison urges, instead, that scriptural descriptions of nature are popular rather than scientific).

Harrison lists three criteria which are important. He would have us remember: (1) that the Bible was written in patterns of thought that represent an Oriental milieu that often differs from our own; (2) that the unity of

[1]Arnold W. Hearn, "Fundamentalist Renascence," *Christian Century* April 30, 1958, p. 528.
[2]Everett F. Harrison, "Criteria of Biblical Inerrancy," *Christianity Today*, January 20, 1958, pp. 14-18.

scriptural truth is not incompatible with diverse biblical statements; (3) that Scripture should be judged in terms of its faithfulness to its intended purpose.

In 1957, Marcius Taber, writing in *The Christian Century,* challenged orthodoxy to substantiate what he believed to be the two major assumptions behind its approach to the Bible. He claimed that —

> These assumptions are not examined and cannot be substantiated; yet without them the fundamentalist (and evangelical) position collapses. The first is that human language is of such a nature that it is possible to formulate precise and completely adequate statements concerning the moral, spiritual and metaphysical verities of our universe not only for our contemporaries but for future generations as well. The second is that if God is going to make any significant revelation of himself and his purposes, he must choose to make it by an infallible, verbally inspired document of some sort, such as the Bible and the classical formulations of Christian beliefs. Until both of these assumptions are satisfactorily dealt with, most of the arguments for the fundamentalist position are irrelevant or without substantial foundation.[3]

While Taber's article accurately sketched the problems that face the conservative, his remarks showed a remarkable ignorance of the evangelical literature on the subject. Taber was quite certain that evangelicals had ignored these assumptions. However, two years before his article was published, a dialogue on the nature and reliability of biblical language had already begun in *The Gordon Review.* As to the second assumption (about infallibility), conservative theologians like B. B. Warfield and Henry Preserved Smith had carried on an intense theological debate over the matter at least sixty years before Taber wrote his unfortunate remarks.

In this chapter we shall examine some of evangelicalism's attempts to deal with these problems and notice some of the implications of its thought for the doctrine of biblical inerrancy.

[3]Marcius Taber, "Fundamentalist Logic," *Christian Century,* July 3, 1957, p. 817f.

I. The Dialogue Over the Semantics of Biblical Language

Semantics is the study of the relationship between language and meaning. A problem arises from the fact that there is seldom any resemblance between the signs or symbols used in a language and the interpretation or understanding of those signs. The mind must interpret the symbols correctly before meaning can be conveyed.

A. "Inerrancy" or "Adequacy"

A few years ago, Dr. Eugene Nida asked the following questions in *The Gordon Review*: "What is the relationship between the Bible and the Word of God? To what extent may divine communication be non-verbal? How may word symbols which have particular meaning within the language of revelation be properly translated into another language, in which there are no exact equivalents?"[4]

Missionaries, attempting to translate the message of the Bible into the languages of other cultures, have been perplexed by a series of difficulties. For one thing, no one word ever means the same to two people; even worse is the fact that no two words in the same language ever have exactly the same meaning; and worst of all, no words in any two or more different languages ever mean exactly the same thing. The meaning of words is always determined or influenced by the cultural background of the people who use them. The problem for translators of the Bible is this: granting that the original manuscripts of Scripture are inspired and even inerrant, how can one possibly convey the *identical* meaning in another language (or even in the same language)?

Richard K. Curtis has defended a position which many evangelicals have considered too extreme. However, his remarks have served to balance the views of some whose positions in this regard have been philosophically and theologically naive. Curtis has pointed out that due to the

[4]Eugene Nida, "Language, Culture and Theology," *Gordon Review*, December, 1957, p. 153.

complex problems of language, communication of any kind must be merely satisfied to establish the same link in a chain of associations of things with words so that there are elicited corresponding, though not exactly alike, responses. Due to the difficulties of translating the Scriptures from one language to another and from one culture to another, Curtis suggests that we cannot say that the Bible *as we have it* is the "absolute" Word of God. It merely represents "the original revelation . . . . to a high degree of probability."[5] Curtis states that the only absolute in Christianity is the Triune God. Language is only arbitrary, conventionalized symbolization which is subject to constant change. He asks, therefore, "Would not *adequacy* be a more meaningful designation than 'inerrancy' or 'infallibility' "[6] of the revelation in the Scriptures?

If Curtis intends his remarks to be applicable to the actual truth and reliability of the autographs, his argument is invalid for reasons which we shall notice later. However, if I understand him correctly, it is not his direct intention to deny the concept of biblical inerrancy. By this I mean that his argument still leaves it an open question as to whether or not the autographs were inerrant. Whatever problems and difficulties we face in translating and explaining the original message does not affect the essential reliability nor even the "inerrancy" of that message. Thus, the disjunction which heads this discussion ("inerrancy" or "adequacy") need not be regarded as exclusive. The autographs may have been *inerrant* while later translations and versions are adequate, albeit not perfect, representations of the original message.

Perhaps the greatest difficulty that evangelical theologians must face in their attempt to solve such problems as this is the intense amount of opposition raised by other conservatives. Many fundamentalists seem to think that the truth of God is better off when the problems related to the

5Richard K. Curtis, "Language and Theory," *Gordon Review*, September, 1955, p. 107.
6Richard K. Curtis, *The New Evangelicalism*, (unpublished paper) Bethel College and Seminary, p 7.

justification of that truth are ignored. Many fundamentalists evidence an apparent psychological block against any re-thinking of the problems related to the inerrancy of Scripture. Eugene Nida suggests a possible reason for this opposition:

> In attempting to understand the problem of non-absolute communication we often suffer from certain emotional attitudes which tend to color our thinking, for we have become so familiar with, and confident of, our creedal formulations that we regard any suggestion as to their non-absolute character as being a reflection upon God Himself.[7]

However, most evangelicals recognize that this problem should not and need not affect the doctrine of inerrancy. As Nida put it, "The fact that the linguistic forms of our doctrinal statements cannot be regarded as absolute does not mean that they are incapable of revealing truth about an absolute God."[8]

A number of evangelicals have suggested that much of the psychological opposition to such discussions would be eliminated if people would keep in mind the distinction between what philosophers call logical certainty and moral certainty, that is, the difference between the kind of certainty found in deductive reasoning and the psychological certainty that results from the assurance of faith.

> While by faith we believe in the absolute authority of the Word of God, yet when we approach the problem from the perspective of logical verification we are limited to the area of probability. What we may believe as Christians as certainty can only be demonstrated logically as probability. Hence, this problem of relativity is always with us because of the fact that the revelation of God is involved in history.[9]

B. Propositional Revelation or Personal Revelation

Neo-orthodoxy has also noticed the difficulties involved in any attempt to communicate truth by means of language. However, it has attempted to use this problem as a basis or justification for its peculiar doctrines about the nature of

[7]Nida, op. cit., p. 159.
[8]Ibid.
[9]Warren C. Young, "Whither Evangelicalism?", Bulletin of Evangelical Theological Society, Winter, 1959, p. 11.

revelation. Thus, while both the evangelical and neo-orthodox recognize this problem, their different attitudes toward and answers for the difficulty once again make clear the significant differences that exist between these two schools of thought. The evangelical does not believe the problem of semantics militates against the doctrine of inerrancy, while the neo-orthodox theologian does. In fact, the adherents of the latter position attempt to argue on the basis of this question that propositional revelation is impossible.

William Hordern has, perhaps, stated the neo-orthodox attitude on this point most clearly. First, he claims that it is irrelevant to speak of any "infallible" (I am sure he also has inerrancy in mind) message issuing from a speaker unless that message comes "into the understanding of the hearer meaning precisely (sic) what the speaker meant by them."[10] In other words, one should not say that the Bible itself is "infallible" unless the message of the Bible is understood exactly by the one who reads or hears it. Secondly, Hordern suggests that all of this "nonsense" about an infallible Bible is due to one fundamental error of all conservatives, namely, their insistence that God reveals truth. He argues that we ought to dispense with our belief in such a concept and recognize that revelation is not concerned with propositions at all. Rather, Hordern tells us, God reveals Himself and nothing more. In other words, the content of revelation is not some truth or doctrine *about* God. It is, instead, God's revelation of Himself.

I suggest that we are now at an important crossroad. Fundamentalists have repeatedly asserted that evangelicalism is conceding too much to neo-orthodoxy. Here is the point on which we shall either have to acquiesce to their claims or silence them forever, for in many ways the denial of propositional revelation is *the* cornerstone of neo-orthodox theology. Have the evangelicals capitulated and weakened their stand or have they responded to the challenge with a

[10]William Hordern, *Case for a New Reformation Theology*, Philadelphia, Westminster Press, 1959, p. 59.

clear and forthright defense of propositional revelation? We believe that there can be no doubt but that the latter is the case. As an example, we cite the following arguments of Kenneth Pike which were published in *Christianity Today*, the leading evangelical publication.

In his examination of Hordern's argument, Pike believes that he has found two key assumptions which are fundamental to his position. Hordern's first assumption is that if language is to be true, it must be received as well as given. It is ridiculous, Hordern believes, to claim that a statement or document is "infallible" when *given* unless it is "infallibly interpreted" and thus still infallible when *received*.

Hordern's mistake, according to Pike, is his failure to recognize that language has more functions than simply linking the ideas of one person to the ideas of another. Pike also is convinced that Hordern makes the mistake of confusing the *reliability of a source* of information with the possible *unreliability of the receiver*. Pike's remarks on this matter are most helpful.

> Let us assume, for example, that a teacher of very great scientific competence gives a lecture today to an audience of young graduate students. A tape recording is made of the lecture. Members of the class are asked to comment on or to repeat the day's lecture. Let us suppose that none of them understood the lecture. From the point of view of Hordern, this would not be mere failure to understand truth — it would be evidence that the lecture was *not inerrant*, specifically, and by implication would also be evidence that the lecture is *not wholly true*.

> Three years after, when these same students have had further training, they listen to the old tape again. They now understand it. The material, which formerly was not truth, by Hordern's treatment would now become truth because it would have done what propositions are meant to do.

> In order to avoid this conclusion, I would claim, on the contrary, that the initial lecture was in fact *true*, and was in principle *available*. It needed, however, *prepared receivers* for its adequate reception.[11]

[11]Kenneth L. Pike, "Language and Meaning: Strange Dimensions of Truth," *Christianity Today*, May 8, 1961, p. 691.

It looks very much, then, as if Hordern has made the profound mistake of confusing the simple distinction between *truth* and the *understanding* of truth.

Pike goes on to point out that Hordern's second assumption is that "ambiguity in a statement implies error in the statement itself."[12] Pike's reply to this is that Hordern's conclusion, if accepted, would make all knowledge impossible, for then no statement about anything could ever be true. Take, as an example, the language of science. The meaning of its words are not always as univocal as scientists would have us believe. Since scientific statements must also be analyzed and understood and since they are often misunderstood, it would seem that Hordern has ruled out the possibility of any completely true science. Pike's criticism is indeed sharp as he argues,

> The turn of the wheel is curiously complete. Having, along with the liberals, rejected fundamentalism because "it seemed to require intellectual hari-kari" . . . in its relationships to science, etc. . . . Hordern has in fact adopted a position which, in my view, in turn breeds intellectual hari-kari through denying full truth value to any of the statements or summaries or propositions of science.[13]

Pike concludes his helpful article by offering some distinctions which he believes will help avoid the skeptical implications of Hordern's position. Pike suggests that we recognize that statements contain what he calls *dimensions*. He distinguishes three of them:

(1) Sentences contain the Dimension of Truth versus Error. His point here is that factual (or what the philosopher calls synthetic) statements are always probability statements fluctuating between the two poles of truth and error. Propositions are more probably true or false depending upon their actual correspondence to reality. Thus it is totally absurd to look for logical certainty in any factual statement, even a religiously oriented statement. But it is even more absurd to argue that because the factual state-

[12]*Ibid.*
[13]*Ibid.*, p. 691f.

ments of, for example, the Bible do not possess logical certainty that they, therefore, are not inerrant.

(2) Sentences contain the Dimension of Magnification. By this Pike means that sentences differ in degree of detail but this difference is not a matter of truth or falsity. Since both ultimate pattern and infinite detail can hardly be presented to man at once, one must choose the degree of magnification he wishes to use. Science attempts to reach high magnification, i.e., infinite detail. Pike claims that the Bible uses low magnification in order to make the basic patterns more clear. This necessarily involves an ignoring of much detail.

(3) Sentences contain the Dimension of Relevance, i.e., contexts not only change meaning but also force a selection of meanings that are relevant to the particular intention of the writer.

Thus, Pike's argument is that factual (or synthetic) assertions are subject to probability, leave out some detail in order to show the general pattern and change meaning according to the intention of the speaker. But these are not sufficient reasons to conclude the impossibility of either biblical inerrancy or propositional revelation.

In order to show that Pike's remarks are not those of one "crying in the wilderness," it should be understood that many other evangelicals have objected to the disjunction between propositional and personal revelation. For example, Bernard Ramm writes,

> Some theologians define revelation as the disclosure of a Person and not of truths. But what does it mean to disclose a Person? Certainly two people who are deaf, blind and mute can hardly have any real encounter with each other apart from touch. Real encounter in life between persons is *always within the context of mutual knowledge.* This *mutual knowledge* is not opposed to the encounter, *but it is its indispensable instrument.* The richness of love between a happily married couple cannot be exhaustively reduced to a set of propositions; but that such a rich love could come into being independently of mutual knowledge is absolutely impossible. Therefore, to speak of revelation of a Person and not of truths is to speak — at least from

the analogy of human encounter — nonsense . . . . Revelation is event *and* interpretation, encounter and truth a Person *and* knowledge.[14]

In the first section of this chapter we have examined two specious disjunctions: (1) that our present forms of revelation are either inerrant or adequate; (2) that revelation is either personal or propositional. Evangelicals have argued that these disjunctions are not exclusive. They have insisted *both* that the autographs are inerrant and that our present versions are adequate; they have contended that revelation is *both* personal and propositional. We conclude, then, that on at least these issues evangelical theology shows no affinities to neo-orthodoxy. However, we must now turn our attention to another problem, one which in fact is more complicated.

II. THE DIALOGUE OVER THE FUNCTION OF BIBLICAL LANGUAGE

Edward John Carnell has put his finger on what is probably the basic problem that evangelicals must face in regard to the doctrine of inerrancy. He recalls a nineteenth-century controversy over this matter that occurred within orthodoxy. The contending factions were led by Charles Hodge and B. B. Warfield on the one side and James Orr and Henry Preserved Smith on the other. As Carnell notes, "This protracted exchange of convictions was possibly the last great dialogue on inspiration in America."[15]

The real basis of their disagreement was a difference of opinion over the essential purpose of Scripture. Hodge and Warfield insisted that the primary purpose of the Bible was the communication of truth. This led them to assert, "A proved error in Scripture contradicts not only our doctrine, but the Scripture claims, and therefore its inspiration, in making those claims."[16] It is important to notice here

[14]Bernard Ramm, *Special Revelation and the Word of God*, Grand Rapids, Eerdmans (c. 1961) p. 159f.

[15]Edward John Carnell, *Case for Orthodox Theology*, Philadelphia, Westminster Press, 1959, p. 102.

[16]Everett F. Harrison, "The Phenomena of Scripture," *Revelation and the Bible*, ed. by Carl Henry, Grand Rapids, Baker Book House (c. 1958) p. 238.

that the validity of their argument seemed to rest on their equating inspiration and inerrancy.

James Orr disagreed. He was convinced that the primary purpose of Scripture was the impartation of *life*, not truth. God is more concerned to make us wise unto salvation than to give us an infallible record of the history of the Jewish kings. The reader will make a mistake if he interprets the dispute between Orr and Warfield as an *either-or* situation. The variance was not over whether Scripture communicates *only* truth or *only* life. This, we suggest, would be a specious disjunction like those we noticed earlier in this chapter. Certainly, Scripture is concerned to communicate both truth and life. Truth is the necessary condition for receiving eternal life, while the presence of eternal life is testimony to the fact that God's truth has been received. The dispute, then, was over the *primary* function of revelation — truth (e.g., about the history of Jewish kings) or life! However, Orr did admit the possibility that the Bible contained some historical errors.

Both schools of thought offered arguments to support their points of view. Hodge and Warfield appealed to the numerous verses in the Bible that taught inspiration. The difficulty of their argument was, of course, that plenary inspiration and inerrancy are two different matters. Thus, proof texts for the one are not necessarily proof texts for the other. Henry Preserved Smith pointed to the great problems to which Warfield's doctrine seemed to lead.[17] For example, he offered the case of the speeches of Job's friends which no Christian would regard as containing inerrant truth. In this case, Hodge's position seemed to commit orthodoxy to "saying that inspiration . . . . ensures no more than an infallible account of error."[18]

[17]Perhaps we should point out that some have questioned the accuracy of Carnell's report of the dispute. Dr. J. O. Buswell, Jr. has objected to Carnell's attempt to create a break between the thought of Smith and Hodge, especially with regard to the numbers of the kings. He argues that with but one exception, the cases Carnell cites contain textual problems. Buswell admonishes Carnell for condemning "Warfield for not answering these charges of Smith, but Carnell does not study them out to answer them himself. And this is too bad, for they can be answered." (*Bible Presbyterian Reporter*, Dec. 1959).

[18]Carnell, *op. cit.*, p. 102f.

Carnell reports that "The dialogue between Orr and the Princeton theology was never successfully terminated. The problem of inspiration is *still* a problem."[19] He warns,

> What was once a live issue in the church has now ossified into a theological tradition. As a result a heavy pall of fear hangs over the academic community. When a gifted professor tries to interact with the critical difficulties in the text, he is charged with disaffection, if not outright heresy. Orthodoxy forgets one important verdict of history: namely, that when truth is presented in a poor light, tomorrow's leaders may embrace error on the single reason that it is more persuasively defended.[20]

Carnell believes that this problem deserves a theological "airing out." Although it is often taken for granted that there is nothing more to be said concerning the inspiration and inerrancy of the Bible, Carnell has pointed to an historic example that suggests that in the past (in fact, within the last century) orthodoxy has regarded the matter as still being a somewhat open question. Instead of conservatives uncritically accepting the doctrine as a closed or "ossified theological tradition," Carnell believes that it should once again become a live issue.

Unfortunately, many have misunderstood Carnell and have assumed that he prefers the position of Orr to that of Warfield and, thus, believes that there are errors in Scripture. This is not the case, however, for a careful reading of his argument makes it clear that Carnell is dissatisfied with some aspects of both sides of the controversy as it was left by the nineteenth-century protagonists. He chides Warfield for ignoring the many inductive problems but he also takes Orr to task for so readily admitting historical errors in the text. Orr was wrong in accommodating the doctrine of inspiration to the problems. "If orthodoxy were to tolerate such accommodation, it would forfeit the principle by which *any* Christian doctrine is established. This would banish theology to the wastelands of subjectivity."[21]

19*Ibid.*, p. 109.
20*Ibid.*, p. 110.
21*Ibid.*, p. 111.

But on the other hand, Hodge and Warfield should have been willing (on the basis of the mass of inductive evidence) to admit that they had misunderstood the implications of inerrancy. Such an admission, Carnell points out, would not have destroyed the doctrine of inerrancy:

> Orthodoxy would simply shift its conception of the thing signified (i.e., by the doctrine of inerrancy). Just as the inspired author of Job gives an infallible account of what Eliphaz said, so the inspired author of Chronicles gives an infallible account of what was said in the public registers and genealogical lists. At first blush this may seem like a very desperate expedient, but it actually implies no more than a strained use of procedures already at work in orthodoxy. If Hodge and Warfield had honored this as a possibility, they might have avoided their lofty disregard for the inductive difficulties. And if Orr had done likewise, he might have avoided his perilous admission of historical errors in Scripture.[22]

Carnell concludes his discussion with an unequivocal assertion of his own continued belief in the inerrancy of the Bible. In his words, "Orthodoxy's intramural debate on inspiration in no way disturbs the truth of the gospel, and to think that it does is cultic."[23]

In concluding this chapter, let us leave Hodge, Orr and Carnell behind, and summarize what seem to be the most important points that today's evangelicals are insisting on in connection with the doctrine of inerrancy.

(1) Contemporary evangelicals are pointing out that inspiration and inerrancy are not equivalent concepts. There is no intention on their part to deny inerrancy — only to clarify the fact that it is a distinct matter from inspiration. An important implication of this is that one cannot prove inerrancy simply by citing texts that prove inspiration.

(2) The Bible undoubtedly testifies to its own inspiration. Proof texts for this are legion (II Timothy 3:16, 17; II Peter 1:20, 21; etc.). The liberal may be able to assert his unbelief in the inspiration of the Scriptures but he cannot deny the fact that the Bible claims inspiration for itself.

[22]*Ibid.*
[23]*Ibid.*

No evangelical purports to prove that the Bible is the Word of God simply because it says it is. The circularity of this procedure is so obvious as to need no comment. But the evangelical does believe that we should not ignore the Bible's testimony to its own inspiration. It would be exceedingly strange to ascribe divine inspiration to any religious document which did not even bother to claim such authority for itself. And so the evangelical argues that the Bible's claims about itself ought at least to be taken seriously until they can be shown by other means to be either true or false.

(3) Strictly speaking, the Bible does not teach the inerrancy of its original manuscripts. Everett F. Harrison, who adheres to the essentials of orthodox theology, writes,

> Unquestionably the Bible teaches its own inspiration. It is the Book of God. It does not require us to hold inerrancy, *though this is a natural corollary of full inspiration* . . . (inerrancy) remains a conclusion to which devout minds have come because of the divine character of Scripture.[24]

While the Bible assures us again and again of its inspiration, it really says quite nothing about the inerrancy of the original manuscripts. The inerrancy of the autographs is an *assumption* although the evangelical believes that it is an *important assumption*.

(4) It is important to remember the divine order of primacy in the matters of inspiration and inerrancy. The Bible is not inspired because it is inerrant. If anything, its inerrancy is a result of its inspiration. As James Orr wrote,

> It is urged, e.g., that unless we can demonstrate what is called the "inerrancy" of the Biblical record, down even to its minutest details, the whole edifice of belief in revealed religion falls to the ground. This, on the face of it, is a most suicidal position for any defender of revelation to take up. It is certainly a much easier matter to prove the reality of a divine revelation in the history of Israel, or in Christ, than it is to prove the inerrant inspiration of every part of the record through which that revelation has come to us.[25]

[24]Harrison, "The Phenomena of Scripture," *op. cit.*, pp. 250, 238 (italics mine).
[25]James Orr, *Inspiration and Revelation*, Grand Rapids, Eerdmans, 1952, pp. 197, 198.

In this chapter we have surveyed some of the contemporary evangelical discussion on the doctrine of biblical inerrancy. This has not been by any means a complete picture. At the beginning of the chapter, we took notice of Marcius Taber's claim that orthodoxy has yet to see, let alone examine, the assumptions undergirding its belief in errancy. We have shown, I believe, that: (1) Taber was mistaken. Evangelicals have been grappling with these complicated problems for years; (2) evangelicals have shown the difficulties encountered do not justify an abandonment of the doctrine.

Intellectual honesty and respectability are not acquired by ignoring problems. We must follow the "facts" where they lead us and not sift the facts through any sieve of personal preference. Most evangelicals are convinced that a belief in the inerrancy of the original manuscripts is an important and necessary asumption that remains perfectly consistent with what knowledge we do possess.

PART THREE

EVANGELICALISM AND THE CHURCH

Introduction to Part Three:

Evangelicalism and the Church

Evangelicals have given serious consideration to the study of ecclesiology, the doctrine of the Church. They are particularly concerned with such vexing questions as: what is the nature of the Church? What is the basis of fellowship or separation from other groups of professing believers? What should be the relationship between local churches or denominations and such inter-denomination federations as The National Council of Churches?

An important part of the evangelical's attention in this area has been devoted to a criticism of tendencies within fundamentalism which he believes are detrimental to the cause of conservative Christianity. As we shall see, the disagreement between the evangelical and the fundamentalist over such matters as separatism, ecumenicity and cooperative evangelicalism has created some of the sorest points of tension between the two groups.

To Separate or Not to Separate

Orthodoxy believes that its duty is to preach and defend the Gospel of Christ as it is revealed in Scripture. Thus, fundamentalists and evangelists are faced with a problem unknown by the liberal. For if *this* gospel be the true gospel, what common cause can the conservative have with those who preach another gospel? The complicated and thorny question which constantly faces the conservative is, "Should we separate?"

Since the argument of this chapter will be involved and take many turns, it might be good to indicate here something of the direction in which we are heading and the roads we shall take to get there. Our general objective is to notice the evangelical's dissatisfaction with the hyper-separatism so prevalent within fundamentalism and see what his proposals are for relating orthodoxy to the many types of liberalism. Our procedure will be first to examine the position of an orthodox theologian, J. Gresham Machen, whose views might be termed separatist. We believe that Machen has provided the most coherent and logical case for this position. Then we shall see what objections evangelicals have brought against separatism in general. Finally, we shall discuss the policies of evangelicalism in this regard.

It is necessary to justify our choice of Machen since it has been suggested many times that he was neither a fundamentalist (in the strict sense of the word) nor a separatist. I believe that Machen affords us an excellent example in our study of separatism for several reasons:

(1) After fighting for the cause of orthodoxy within the Presbyterian, U.S.A., Church for several years, Machen

finally withdrew from that denomination and from the faculty of its Princeton Seminary and helped organize the Orthodox Presbyterian Church (as it came to be called) and the Westminster Theological Seminary in Philadelphia. I am well aware of the history of Machen's struggles within the Presbyterian, U.S.A., Church and I know of Cornelius Van Til's claim that "Machen's position is not sectarian or separatist."[1] However, unless Van Til is using the word, "separatist," in a sense different from its ordinary usage, I fail to see his point, for nothing can be clearer than that Machen did lead a group of Presbyterian pastors and students to separate themselves from his denomination. Trying to avoid the term, "separatist," by claiming that the U.S.A. Church had become apostate seems to be irrelevant. We are not here involved in making any value judgments as to whether or not it is good or bad to be a separatist. The point is, was Machen in his preaching and practice a separatist? While we recognize that Machen's position is far removed from the extreme practices of contemporary hyperseparatists and while we even concede that he may have had good cause to separate, the fact remains that Machen was a separatist.

(2) Unlike many hyper-separatists of this generation, Machen based his action and his attitudes upon premises which I am inclined to accept as true. This makes a consideration of his beliefs and practices more worthwhile than a study of some contemporary hyper-separatists who do little more than picket Billy Graham meetings and quote the sixth chapter of II Corinthians out of context. But while admitting that the premises of Machen's argument may have been *true*, we may yet have to find his argument *invalid*, i.e., perhaps his conclusion didn't necessarily follow from those premises.

(3) We find Machen to be a good example because after he separated from the U.S.A. Church, a group of his own followers (led by Carl McIntyre) dissented from his

[1]Cornelius Van Til, *The New Evangelicalism*, (unpublished paper) Philadelphia, Westminster Theological Seminary, p. 11.

leadership and split into still a new denomination, The Bible Presbyterian Church. This incident (together with its many parallels in other denominations) lends support to the evangelical contention that perhaps separatism *per se* has not been an intrinsic blessing to orthodoxy.

(4) Finally, we have chosen Machen because Edward John Carnell has subjected Machen and his views to an outspoken criticism in his book, *The Case for Orthodox Theology*. However, the reader should understand that we do not intend simply to retrace the steps of Carnell's presentation. Indeed, we shall find good cause to criticize much of Carnell's argument in this book. Rather, we wish to examine Carnell's criticism for hints it may give us of the evangelical's reasons for dissenting from separatism.

We shall now proceed to our consideration of Machen's position. It is not our purpose to determine whether or not Machen's separation from the Presbyterian U.S.A. Church was justified. Among other things, this would call into question the existence of a denomination that we respect and admire, i.e., The Orthodox Presbyterian Church.

I. Machen's Premises

Machen's chief arguments concerning the nature of Christianity are to be found in his classic exposition of orthodoxy, *What Is Christianity?* He begins by noting that it does little good to study the Christian faith until we first of all determine what Christianity is, that is, we must find out what it is that we are to study. "Christianity" is a name applied to a variety of diverse and even contradictory beliefs. Is Catholicism Christianity, or is Protestantism? How is it that such widely divergent theological tendencies as neo-orthodoxy, fundamentalism, liberalism, unitarianism and even the unscientific pantheism of Mary Baker Eddy have all claimed the title of "Christian"?

Our first task, Machen advises us, is to define Christianity. However, we must be careful not to arbitrarily define the faith as we please. Let us not beg the question and define Christianity so that it describes only our particular

kind of religious practice. Let us see if there is some criterion that will enable us to find out what Christianity
really is.

Machen tells us that Christianity "is an historical
phenomenon like the State of Pennsylvania or the U.S.A. . . .
and it must be investigated by historical means."[2] He asks,
to what point in the "long history of Christianity should we
turn in order to discover what it really is?" His answer is,
"To the beginnings of the movement."

What is America? The answer to that is found in the
Constitution and the Bill of Rights. Since America was
founded, we recognize that teachings or practices in this
country that are contrary to these basic documents are
"un-American." This does not mean that we are dictating
to other nations how they should run their internal affairs.
Machen's argument is simply this: to deserve the name
"American," we must act in accordance with those basic
documents.

Machen argues that this is also the case with Christianity. The only way to find out what constitutes Christianity
is to go back to *its* original document. In the words of Gordon
Clark, "Christianity, then, is simply what the Bible teaches."[3]
Machen is not arguing that the early founders of Christianity
had a right to legislate for all subsequent generations. But
they did have a right to legislate for all subsequent generations choosing to bear the name, "Christian." He
argues that if we change their program or beliefs, we should
have the honesty to change the name. "It is misleading (and
dishonest?) to use the old name to designate a new thing."

But this is the very thing which many varieties of
theology in Christendom will not do. They want to claim
that Christianity is properly understood to mean whatever
"Christians" today believe and whatever "Christians" today
practice. The reason, we are told, why these beliefs and
practices which may be so divergent from New Testament

[2]J. Gresham Machen, *What Is Christianity?* Grand Rapids, Eerdmans, 1951,
p. 18.
[3]Gordon Clark, *Christian View of Men and Things,* Grand Rapids, Eerdmans, 1951, p. 83.

days may still be called Christian is because of the historical and cultural tie that binds them to the early Christian Church.

Gordon Clark repudiates the appeal to historical continuity by contrasting the history of Christianity with the history of Platonism. Plato founded the Academy in Athens. The most important element of his philosophy was the doctrine of the forms, the belief that eternal, absolute and unchanging truth existed in a supersensible world. The Academy lasted for 900 years but within a few centuries of Plato's death, it was no longer following its founder's emphasis on the absoluteness of truth and the importance of knowledge as opposed to opinion. Instead, the Academy had become a hot bed of skepticism. It insisted that it was impossible to attain any truth. Clark comments,

> This skeptical Academy of the second and first centuries was undoubtedly the corporate successor to Plato and his pupils. There had been an unbroken continuity. But to call their skeptical views Platonism would empty the word of all meaning. . . . Platonism is a definite theory of Ideas. Wherever that theory is found, with or without institutional continuity, it is Platonism; and wherever it is not found, particularly wherever skepticism is professed, there is no Platonism, no matter how strict the apostolic succession.
>
> Similarly, if the term Christianity is to have any definite meaning, if it is not to be applied to theories or to manners of life that are in direct opposition to each other, some criterion must be chosen other than the historical continuity of social groups.[4]

It might be good here to anticipate several possible misunderstandings of or objections to what has already been said. First, was Machen setting himself up as an authority or judge over all other Christians? Was he assuming the right to decide who was and who was not a Christian? I shall allow Machen to answer this himself:

> We are not dealing with delicate personal questions: we are not presuming to say whether such and such an individual man is a Christian or not. God only can decide such questions; no man can say with assurance whether the attitude of certain individual "liberals" toward Christ is saving

4Ibid., p. 82.

faith or not. But one thing is perfectly plain — whether or not liberals are Christians, it is at any rate perfectly clear that liberalism is not Christianity. And that being the case, it is highly undesirable that liberalism and Christianity should continue to be propagated within the bounds of the same organization.[5]

Secondly, was Machen denying liberals the right to construct a modernistic religion? No! On the contrary, he admitted that they had a perfect right to construct any religion they chose. His point, however, was that they had no right to call that religion Christianity if it contradicted the "original documents" of the Faith. Machen believed that the liberal could not be honest, for to be so would mean that he, i.e., the liberal, would have to withdraw from the confessional churches and thus "sacrifice the opportunity . . . of so obtaining control of those confessional churches as to change their fundamental character . . . ."[6] Machen's forthright conclusion was that Christianity is the religion taught in the Bible and none other. Of course, he recognized that there are differences of interpretation of the Bible. But these differences will always be much less than the difficulties encountered by allowing the name of Christianity to be applied to every Tom-Dick-and-Harry theology that desires it.

> Is it not similarly the scholarly thing to do to work out the detailed exposition of Christianity by a careful study of the text? The difficulties should not be minimized; but neither should the responsibility be shirked, for only by this method can the contradictions and confusions of contemporary statements be authoritatively evaluated.[7]

Such then was Machen's argument and I take it that it was a good one. In fact, even Edward John Carnell agreed (in 1954) with Walter Lippman that "The liberals have yet to answer Dr. Machen."[8] But the evangelical is concerned to ask several questions at this point:

[5]J. Gresham Machen, *Christianity and Liberalism*, Grand Rapids, Eerdmans, 1923, p. 160.
[6]*Ibid.*, p. 165.
[7]Clark, *op. cit.*, p. 84.
[8]E. J. Carnell, *Theology of Reinhold Niebuhr*, Grand Rapids, Eerdmans, 1954, p. 24.

(1) Does Machen's view concerning the nature of the Church necessarily imply the need of separation? Machen evidently believed that it did. As Machen's present day counsel for defense, Van Til, puts it:

> If anything was clear to Machen it was that schism is sin. But he also knew that there were those in the church of his youth who in effect denied the Christ on whom the church is founded. When the church no longer proclaimed the substitutionary death of Christ as central to its teaching it was no longer the church of Christ.[9]

Perhaps this question should be put another way. Might it ever be the case that the Christian, while despairing of liberal tendencies within his denomination, would draw back from separation realizing that it could possibly do more harm in the long run than good? We are not suggesting that separation is never justified. Indeed, we believe that times have undoubtedly arisen when separation was definitely required. For those who wish an example, one need only point to Luther and the Reformation.

Even Van Til himself lends an unwitting support to our suggestion that Machen's premises may not always necessitate separation. For Van Til and other defenders of Machen repeatedly remind us that there is just as much reason to believe that the circumstances in which Machen found himself were more responsible for his final decision to leave his denomination than anything else. In other words, had it not been for the unfortunate attempt to try Machen in a church court, he might not have been so quick to make his final break. I am suggesting, then, that in Machen's case, his separation was based on more than doctrinal disagreements.

(2) Was there any possible connection between Machen's act of separation and the troubles that later plagued his denomination? For Carl McIntyre and a small group of pastors and students separated themselves from Machen's fellowship and began the Bible Presbyterian Church and Faith Theological Seminary. The issue this time was not orthodoxy, but, among other things, dispensa-

[9]Van Til, *op. cit.* p. 10.

tionalism and eschatology. Carnell believes that this was a fitting judgment on Machen's theories.

> Machen . . . honored Reformed doctrine, but not the Reformed doctrine of the church. This inconsistency had at least two effects: First, it encouraged Machen's disciples to think that the conditions of Christian fellowship could be decided by subjective criteria; secondly, it planted the seeds of anarchy . . . The result was a subtle reversion to the age of the Judges: each man did what was right in his own eyes.[10]

However, the evangelical looks beyond the divisions that followed Machen's break to the multiple schisms and divisions that have rent orthodoxy since the 1930's. For when the fundamentalist found that he no longer had any more liberals to separate himself from, he began to find issues to dispute which he could use to justify his separation from conservative brethren. Evangelicals are beginning to wonder out loud whether there is any relationship between the spirit of separatism and the spirit of independency and censoriousness that presently plagues conservative Christianity.

II. CARNELL'S CRITICISM OF MACHEN

We remarked earlier that Carnell has criticized separatism in general and Machen in particular in his book, *The Case for Orthodox Theology*. We now wish to examine some of the things he said. It is not our intent simply to reiterate his argument, for we believe that Carnell's position as he set it forth in his *Case* is inadequate for at least three reasons: First, he failed to make really clear just what it was that the evangelical was objecting to; secondly, he failed to state adequately the positive evangelical goals and methods; and thirdly, his remarks have consequently produced much misunderstanding of the evangelical position.

A. Carnell's Criticism of Machen Is Not Clear

Carnell succeeded in showing everyone that evangelicals are not as happy with separatism as they could be. But

[10]Carnell, *Case, op. cit.,* p. 117.

he did not adequately state why. Since we shall attempt to furnish these reasons later, we shall pass this by for now.

B. Carnell's Case for His Own Position Is Deficient

Near the end of his book, Carnell urged orthodoxy to "return to the classical view of the Church." However, it should be noted that in no sense of the word did Carnell tell us what that classical view of the church is. What he did do was lay down several principles for the Christian to follow:

"First: all other things being equal, a Christian should remain in the fellowship that gave him spiritual birth."[11] Unfortunately, the qualification, "all other things being equal," seems to be a subtle appeal to the same kind of subjective criteria for Christian fellowship that Carnell found so offensive in Machen's thought.

"Secondly: A Christian should judge the claims of a church by its official creed or confession, not by the lives of its members."[12] Here, Carnell seems to oversimplify what is an exceedingly complicated situation. He seems, in fact, to be condoning a maxim of the nature, "Don't do what I do, do what I say." It apparently didn't bother Carnell when he wrote these words if a church or members within a denomination did not believe its creed.[13] Is the conservative supposed to bury his head in the sand and say, "Of course, we both know that you don't really believe this creed but as long as you make a pretense of believing it, I'll go along with you"? Carnell seems to think that the conservative should be satisfied if he is free to preach *his* gospel and free to protest against abuses. But the question goes deeper than this. Is the conservative only preaching *his* gospel or *the* gospel?

"Thirdly: Separation from an existing denomination is justifiable on only two criteria. a. Eviction . . . b. apostasy."[14] The first criterion is scarcely worth noticing. It goes without

---

[11]*Ibid.*, p. 133.
[12]*Ibid.* p. 134.
[13]But we shall suggest, shortly, that Carnell does seem to have changed his mind on this point.
[14]*Ibid.*, pp. 136, 137.

saying that if a conservative is *evicted* from a denomination that he is *separated* from it. This is pure tautology. The more important criterion is apostasy, but Carnell disappoints us when he comes to explain what constitutes this apostasy. He writes, "If a denomination removes the gospel from its creed or confessions, or if it leaves the gospel (sic - what gospel?) but removes the believer's right to preach it, the believer may justly conclude that the denomination is apostate."[15]

C. Van Til's Criticism of Carnell

Many have found Carnell's remarks deficient and equivocal. Unfortunately, they have concluded that Carnell's statements in *The Case* are always representative of all evangelicals. This has led to numerous misunderstandings and a host of ungrounded objections.

If one takes Carnell's position to be what he implies in *The Case*, then Cornelius Van Til seems to be right when he says,

> Carnell defines the church as "a fellowship of all who share in the blessings of the Abrahamic covenant." But those who deny the once-for-all character of the atonement wrought by him on whom all the promises of Abraham terminate can scarcely be said to share in the blessing of the Abrahamic covenant.[16]

Furthermore, Carnell did give the impression (although we shall notice that in a later writing, he attempts to remove it) that the evangelical is apparently willing to overlook unbelief. Nothing could possibly be further from the true evangelical position, but nonetheless Carnell succeeded in convincing Van Til that the evangelical doctrine of the Church involves "doctrinal indifferentism." Van Til believes that Carnell no longer views the Church as —

> composed of those who accept, *ex animo,* the Christ of the Scriptures. If the Reformers had held the view of the church as entertained by Carnell there would have been no reformation. The church as constituted at the time of Luther and Calvin had not departed as far from the Christ of the Scriptures as did the church of Machen's time.[17]

15*Ibid.*, p. 137.
16Van Til, *New Evangelicalism, op. cit.*, p. 12.
17*Ibid.*, p. 11.

We are suggesting then that Carnell's criticism of Machen and separatism as found in *The Case for Orthodox Theology* has created confusion both about his actual point of view and also about the position of evangelicalism. Our task in the remainder of this chapter, then, must be to clear up this confusion.

III. Evangelicalism and Separation

A. *Evangelical Objections to Separatism*

First, let it be said that evangelicalism is not opposed to separatism *per se*. There may be and undoubtedly have been times when separation from theological apostasy has been more than justified. But, the evangelical asks, has twentieth-century separatism done what it set out to do, namely, keep the Church of Christ pure? The evangelical thinks not and offers in support of his contention the following evidence:

(1) Twentieth-century separatism has tended to foster divisive attitudes within orthodoxy. No one objects to the conservative's right to disagree and even dissent from liberalism. The trouble comes when men fail to stop there and carry their divisive tendencies into their conduct toward other brethren. One of the prime "virtues" of the twentieth-century separatist is theological pugnaciousness. One can hear them speak proudly and boastfully of their "militant fundamentalism," "uncompromising fundamentalism," "fighting fundamentalism," and so on, *ad nauseam*. The trouble is that these men are often refusing to compromise on issues that are of secondary importance and the people they are fighting are often those who simply refuse to follow their acceptance of these minor issues. When there are no more liberals within range, they don't stop fighting. The issues simply change. So they now challenge all those who refuse to concur with their belief, for example, that the rapture takes place before the tribulation. Their mottos become, "Holding forth the Word of Strife," or "Rightly dividing the Church of God." Vernon Grounds has described such men as fundamentalists with a "theological chip" on

their shoulders. While the evangelical is as anxious to defend the great verities of the Christian faith as any fundamentalist, he believes that this can be done with a measure of Christian grace and courtesy.

(2) Twentieth-century separatism has exalted minor doctrines unduly and made them tests of fellowship. Carl Henry tells us that this "spirit of independency" has continued to incorporate "secondary doctrines into its creed with an absoluteness that is incredible." He adds that as separatism "moves in the direction of Pharisaism, man-made appendages to the Gospel become all-important, constituting a test for fellowship. Not one's belief in Christ as God and Savior, but whether one sits in the right millenial pew and properly dots every 'i' and crosses every 't' according to the approved subsidiary requirements is determinative."[18]

Edward John Carnell (in a book written after his *Case*) notes that the separatist ignores the scriptural basis for fellowship and exalts his own:

> Jesus himself was the rallying point for fellowship, doctrine, and form: *fellowship* because the mourners were bound by cords of love; *doctrine* because the teaching of the Lord was normative; and *form* because the will of the Lord became the will of the group . . . The believers knew that if they failed to love one another, their profession in doctrine and form would profit nothing.[19]

Carnell then goes on to show how the fundamentalist is only following in the footsteps of others in the history of the Church who have ignored the scriptural basis of Christian fellowship and elevated their own. Whenever this happened, the Church became afflicted with divisions. For example, Roman Catholicism exalted the *form* of the Church over fellowship and doctrine so that even if an individual (like Luther) believed the Scriptures and trusted in Christ, he fell short of *Catholic standards*. But then Luther exalted his form of communion over fellowship and doctrine so that even though, for example, an Anabaptist believed the Scrip-

[18]Carl Henry, "The Perils of Independency," *Christianity Today*, Nov. 12, 1956, pp. 20, 22.
[19]E. J. Carnell, *The Kingdom of Love and the Pride of Life*, Grand Rapids, Eerdmans (c. 1960) p. 110.

tures and received Jesus as Lord and Savior, he still fell short of *Luther's standards.* John Calvin elevated doctrine (that of election) over fellowship so that an Arminian could believe the Scriptures and receive Jesus as Lord and Savior and still fall short of *Calvin's standards.* The Anglicans exalted the established church over fellowship so that regenerated non-conformists fell short of *Anglican standards.* And such, too, was the case with the Scotch Presbyterians, the Puritans, Methodists, Baptists, Congregationalists. And such is the case with the twentieth-century separatists. The evangelical is protesting, then, against those who today split the Church of Christ and separate themselves from believers who will not measure up to *their standards!*

(3) Twentieth-century separatism has failed or refused to communicate with those theologians with whom it disagrees. This has not only resulted in a common attitude of rudeness and censoriousness on the part of many fundamentalists, but has also helped contribute to many of liberalism's misunderstandings of just what it is that orthodoxy believes. A case in point would be the widespread ignorance of the orthodox view of inspiration that we pointed out in an earlier chapter.

Recently a storm of protest was raised because a certain evangelical seminary invited a liberal to speak to its students. A group of fundamentalists objected, accused the seminary of becoming liberal, and urged Christians to withdraw their support of this school. We think that this action illustrates one of the worst characteristics of contemporary fundamentalism. Certainly such a practice does not necessarily honor the man invited to speak and the seminary made it very clear in public announcements that its action was in no way an endorsement of the man's theological position. If one of the protesting fundamentalists should ever be invited to speak at a liberal seminary, we would hope that he would have enough sense not to be deceived into thinking that *that* seminary had suddenly become conservative and was therefore endorsing his fundamentalism! Sound education demands a fair presentation of contending views. This writer is only too familiar with many so-called "liberal" schools where the orthodox viewpoint is dismissed without a fair hearing, whereas numerous evangelical institutions, while careful to point out the weaknesses, make an earnest effort to present as objectively as possible the liberal position. Evangelicals are concerned to avoid both the bias of many liberal schools and the obscurantism of many fundamentalist institutions, while at the same time presenting and defending the truth of God as they see it.

(4) Twentieth-century separatism has undoubtedly contributed to the individualism and self-seeking that seems to characterize some fundamentalist leaders. Carnell has obviously met some of these men whom he caricaturizes as saying,

> Things are in terrible shape; errorists are everywhere. The true faith is being threatened; my own life is in danger. Something must be done; some courageous person must volunteer. I'm free; I'm ready; I'm willing . . . Oh, yes, you may subscribe to my paper and keep up with the *real* truth. Three dollars will enroll you in my movement, and for $5.00 you may have a copy of my latest book.[20]

As one disheartened conservative recently put it, fundamentalism and separatism have reached the place where they have too many chiefs and too few Indians.

(5) Evangelicalism accuses twentieth-century separatism of departing from the New Testament doctrine of the Church, particularly, its teaching of the organic and spiritual unity of the Body of Christ.

(6) Twentieth-century separatism must take much of the blame for orthodoxy's surrender of many large areas of Christendom to liberalism. The separatists left whole denominations, together with their seminaries, churches and agencies, in the hands of the liberals. We are not denying that at the time of withdrawal the liberals were in control of these things. But does that mean that every time that the balance of power swings away from us that we should cease being a minority voice? Does this warrant our surrender of the *whole* every time the liberals are in the

20Carnell, *Case, op. cit.,* p. 119.

majority? Now, thirty years later, orthodoxy has little voice within many of these influential areas of the Church.

B. Evangelical Goals and Methods

Evangelicals have come to believe that orthodoxy has retreated enough. Each time that liberalism came in, conservatives fought a few skirmish battles. Then they headed for the hills and attempted to set up their own strongholds. Evangelicals believe that conservatives as a whole must adopt new attitudes.

Harold John Ockenga has made it clear that one of the primary objectives of evangelicalism is the recapture of "denominational leadership from within the denominations rather than abandoning these denominations to modernism."[21] The strategy or method that Ockenga recommends is "infiltration." He points out that this was the very means the liberals used to gain control of the major religious bodies in the first place. He urges, "It is time for firm evangelicals to seize their opportunity to minister in and influence the modernist groups. Why is it incredible that the evangelicals should be able to infiltrate the denominations and strengthen the things that remain, and possibly resume control of such denominations?"[22]

Certainly there is something to be said for any honest method that might win back denominational control for orthodoxy and thus increase its spiritual impact upon our nation and its culture. We have had over thirty years of separatism, and honesty forces us to admit that its results have not been altogether successful nor honoring to Christ.

But are Machen and the evangelicals really at odds? Machen's arguments dealt with the nature of true Christianity. The evangelical's arguments concern methods that will once again win the day for orthodoxy rather than continue the present day retreat of the separatists. Perhaps the controversy between the separatists and evangelicals is due to their different perspectives. Machen was confronted by the

[21]Harold John Ockenga, "Resurgent Evangelical Leadership," *Christianity Today*, Oct. 10, 1960, p. 14.
[22]*Ibid.*, p. 15.

sorry sight of theological liberalism in the Church. Evangelicals are confronted by the equally sorry sight of ethical indifference in fundamentalism which can be seen in its sectarianism, separatism and total ignoring of the law of love. The evangelical is not afraid or hesitant to fight for his faith, but he wants to make certain that those whom he's fighting are the enemies of the faith, and he wants to be sure that what he's fighting about is a truly essential element of the faith and not some man-made appendage.

But the separatist continues to view the evangelical with suspicion. The fundamentalist is convinced that the evangelical is compromising the faith. We believe, however, that we have offered evidence in this chapter and in this book that this charge cannot be substantiated. The evangelical is as convinced of the veracity of the fundamentals of the faith as ever. The evangelical believes that true Christianity is what the Bible teaches. The evangelical is as against liberalism in its many forms as ever. But he is also unhappy with the extremes of separatism and his efforts should be viewed as an attempt (albeit an admittedly difficult attempt) to maintain a fidelity to the doctrinal verities of the faith without the unfortunate excesses now so common in separatism.

One final word is necessary. We feel it is most necessary to stress the fact that evangelicals are not advocating any kind of "theological indifferentism." Carnell himself has sought to correct this wrong impression in one of his latest books:

> Once we become indifferent to right doctrine, it will not be long before we shall also become indifferent to fit fellowship for the two go together. Saving faith does not take place in a vacuum. It is an act that grows out of a vital response to the gospel, and the gospel is based on specific redemptive events. If we disparage these events, we surrender the normative elements in the Christian religion.[23]

This is not a matter for which there are any easy solutions. Each case has to be examined for its own peculiar problems. But evangelicals are suggesting that serious

[23]Carnell, *Kingdom of Love, op. cit.,* p. 119.

consideration ought to be given before any step is taken toward separation. The problem is complicated by the separatists' viewing of such efforts with suspicion and their prompt withdrawal from the fellowship of such "compromisers." Perhaps the day will come when God will give to His Church not only a love for the truth but a love for other believers as well. Until that day comes, the question of "to separate or not to separate" is going to become an increasingly more serious source of division within orthodoxy.

CHAPTER 7

To Unite or Not to Unite

CHAPTER 7

To Unite or Not to Unite

We have seen that the evangelical is adopting a different attitude toward the problem of separation. But what of his attitude toward cooperation with those of other theological persuasions? Many fundamentalists have jumped to the conclusion that the evangelical's dissatisfaction with hyperseparatism means that he is necessarily committed to full cooperation with liberals. This conclusion, however, is oversimplified and mistaken. In a consideration of evangelical cooperation with liberals, there are two especially important problem areas — that of ecumenicalism and that of cooperative evangelism.

I. PROBLEM AREA NUMBER ONE: ECUMENICALISM

An excellent example of the dual nature of the evangelical position can be seen in two editorials that Carl Henry wrote for the early issues of *Christianity Today*. He warned of both "the perils of independency" as well as "the perils of ecumenicity." Both of these, Henry argued, are extreme movements. The spirit of independency is best exemplified by the extreme right wing of orthodoxy, The American Council of Christian Churches and its offspring, The International Council of Christian Churches. The spirit of ecumenicity (or what Henry also calls the spirit of "organic church unity") is represented by the National and World Council of Churches. Henry believes that each of these two movements —

> has its own tensions and perils. Independency tends to be intolerant, Church Unionism to be tolerant. The former moves in the direction of exclusivism, the latter toward inclusivism. One holds a low view of the Church in its visible and historical aspects, and the other a high view.

101

The one glorifies separateness, while the other reaches out toward ecclesiasticism. Independency remains highly creedal in minute detail, while Church Unionism becomes vague and ill-defined in theological basis. One can easily become Pharisaic, the other Sadducean.[1]

What is the evangelical attitude toward ecumenicity? Does it view church unionism as an intrinsic evil, an intrinsic good, or neither? Is evangelicalism trying to walk a tight-rope beween independency and ecumenicity and, if so, for what reasons? And if it is, may evangelicalism be rightfully accused of possessing a spirit of compromise (in the bad sense of the word)? While there are naturally some disagreements among evangelicals on some points, I believe that most are agreed on the following issues:

A. The Need for Theological Dialogue

Evangelicals are more conscious than fundamentalists of the need to carry on an exchange of ideas with liberal and neo-orthodox theologians. Vernon Grounds has stated that an "evangelical can be organizationally separated from all Christ-denying fellowship and yet profitably engage in an exchange of ideas with men who are not evangelicals."[2] Indeed, unless the conservative does this he is not fulfilling Christ's injunction to carry the Gospel to *all* men.

B. The Need for an Evangelical Definition of Ecumenicity

Advocates of ecumenicity are not always agreed about the nature of the unity they are purportedly seeking. Some give the impression that they will be satisfied with nothing less than a complete organizational unity. More moderate ecumenists believe that the best hope for success lies in the direction of a more spiritual unity. Because of this dichotomy, someone has remarked that ecumenicity is definitely going somewhere — it just doesn't know where.

Evangelicals must be actively engaged in making clear the true and biblical sense of ecumenicity. J. Marcellus

[1]Carl Henry, "The Perils of Independency," *Christianity Today*, Nov. 12, 1956, p. 20.
[2]Quoted by Richard Curtis, *The New Evangelicalism* (unpublished paper), Bethel College and Seminary, Minneapolis, Minn., p. 18.

Kik has given us an example of efforts along this line. He has written,

> Ecumenism is the movement in the universal visible church upon earth by which, under the influence and guidance of the Holy Spirit, the church comes into the unity of the faith and of the knowledge of the Son of God unto the measure of the stature of the fullness of Christ.[3]

Furthermore it is up to the evangelical to protest against the equating of ecumenicity with the concept of a world wide visible church organization. Biblically, at least, the two are not equivalent.

Before we leave this point, we should recognize that there is some conservative dissatisfaction with the evangelical position. Van Til, for example, has complained that beyond the evangelical's criticism of independency and ecumenism,

> . . . there is little in Henry's writings that tells us something of the nature of the church. Presumably his own view of the church resembles that of the Reformed Confessions. But apparently for purposes of getting a hearing for the gospel today by means of a cooperative effort, the Reformed view of the church must not be pushed to the front.[4]

It is easy to understand Van Til's concern. But Henry suggests that perhaps the vagueness that has characterized the evangelical discussion is necessary. He points out that a mediating position —

> . . . is not so easily defined since the lines are not so sharply drawn. It subscribes to some concepts of each of the extremist groups, but opposes others, finding its rationale in a mediating view, or perhaps better described as a perspective above the extremes. Extreme positions are easier to perceive and less difficult to defend to the popular mind. Whether they are truer is a matter for debate.[5]

C. The Need for an Evangelical Critique of Ecumenicity

The evangelical must protest against what he believes to be doctrinal perversions and heterodox tendencies within

[3]J. Marcellus Kik, *Ecumenism and the Evangelical*, Philadelphia, Presbyterian and Reformed, 1958, p. 3.
[4]Van Til, *New Evangelicalism*, *op. cit.*, p. 45.
[5]Henry, "Perils of Independency," *op. cit.*, p. 21.

existing ecumenical movements. At times the evangelical gets the impression that the organic unity sought by the advocates of ecumenicity can only be attained by a theological inclusivism so radical as to remove the distinctives of the Christian Faith. Evangelicals are unhappy with the "doctrinal laxity," "theological vagueness" and "doctrinal inclusivism" so prevalent in The National and World Council of Churches.

Carl Henry accuses ecumenicity of majoring on minors and minoring on majors, that is, it exalts "to a place of primacy what is not important, (while) relegating to a secondary position that which is basic and necessary to a full-orbed Gospel." [6]

The evangelical wonders why the ecumenicist is so quick to appeal to the Bible in support of church unity and even quicker to ignore all the rest that Scripture teaches. Why use the Bible to defend the unity of the Body of Christ and ignore what it says about the Virgin Birth or the bodily resurrection of Christ? "By what logic and authority, then, is there any justification for the isolation of one strand of the Biblical teaching from all else, elevating it to a position of supreme importance and degrading the other teachings to positions of relative inconsequence?"[7]

D. The Need for an Evangelical Alliance

Whatever the evangelical attitude is toward the National Council and the World Council of Churches, one thing remains clear. Conservatives (and by this I mean fundamentalists, evangelicals and the other branches of orthodoxy) ought to realize the importance of uniting among themselves so that they might speak with the authority and influence of a strong and united minority.

We are not necessarily advocating any mergers of orthodox denominations although we believe the differences separating many such groups are often trivial and petty. Edward John Carnell (perhaps to counter the misunderstandings and criticisms of his position in *The Case*) has

[6]Henry, "Perils of Ecumenicity," *Christianity Today*, Nov. 26, 1956, p. 22.
[7]*Ibid.*, p. 20.

given a much more satisfactory treatment of evangelicalism and church union in his book, *The Kingdom of Love and the Pride of Life*. He suggests that when denominational mergers can be effected among Christians *who agree doctrinally* such mergers should be encouraged, But, he warns,

> Merger is not the whole answer. For one thing, it may serve as a substitute for individual responsibility. Shrinking the number of denominations is no blessing *per se*. Christ prayed for unity, but not for organizational unity. He prayed that his followers might be one, even as the Father and the Son are one. This implies a *vital* unity, and vital unity implies fellowship. Thus, if organizational merger detracts Christians from their obligation to love another, it is a hindrance to unity, not an encouragement.[8]

Fundamentalists should notice that this hardly sounds like a plea for indiscriminate church unionism or "doctrinal indifferentism." Carnell goes on to make it clear that Christians will naturally disagree over such controversial items as church government, communion, baptism, sanctification and predestination. "We should not be ashamed of our theological differences. They are signs that we are taking the work of exegesis seriously. Furthermore, a genuine Christian fellowship can exist *within* the framework of denominational plurality. Love can hurdle existing barriers."[9]

One of the more important factors that explains the growth and success of liberalism may be the fact that liberals have learned that united they stand and divided they fall. A long time ago Jesus warned that "Every city or house divided against itself shall not stand." While His remarks were meant for a different context, they apply equally as well to the present state of orthodox theology.

E. Conclusion

The evangelical attitude toward ecumenicity is not an easy thing to define. This is largely due to its being a mediating position that attempts to transcend the perspectives of

8E. J. Carnell, *Kingdom of Love and the Pride of Life*, Grand Rapids, Eerdmans (c. 1960) p. 118.
9*Ibid.*, p. 119.

both independency and church unionism. On the one hand, evangelicalism wants freedom to converse with liberals while on the other hand it maintains the right to criticize. On the one hand, evangelicalism wants fellowship with other conservative brethren but it also wants the right to warn against the dangers of the spirit of independency. Realizing that there ought to be a conservative voice within, e.g., The World Council of Churches, the evangelical is also aware of the primary need of uniting the many contending segments of orthodoxy. Unfortunately, the measures that evangelicals have adopted to accomplish these things have only widened the breach between them and, for example, the fundamentalists. Due to the mistakes of the evangelicals (for they have made many), the obstinancy of the fundamentalists and the parochial opinions of other conservatives like Van Til, orthodoxy is a long way from any satisfactory answer to these problems.

II. PROBLEM AREA NUMBER TWO:
COOPERATIVE EVANGELISM

Perhaps the most tragic example of the disagreement existing between evangelicalism and fundamentalism to be found is the varied attitudes toward the evangelistic ministry of Billy Graham. One of the strangest and saddest results of Graham's New York campaign was the criticism that came directly from the fundamentalists. *The Sword of the Lord,* a fundamentalist weekly, has accused Graham of being the "principal sparkplug of a great drift away from strict Bible fundamentalism . . . . The New York Crusade has set back the cause of evangelism for at least fifty years."[10] Graham's "great heresy," according to the separatists, is that he preaches the Gospel in campaigns that are often supported by liberal pastors.

In a book entitled *Cooperative Evangelism,* Robert Ferm has attempted to offer evidence from both Scripture (he cites chiefly the methods of Jesus and Paul) and history that Graham's methods are neither unbiblical nor markedly

[10]Quoted by Robert Ferm, *Cooperative Evangelism,* Grand Rapids, Zondervan (c. 1958) pp. 18, 15.

different from those of other great evangelists such as Jonathan Edward, John Wesley, Charles Finney, D. L. Moody and Billy Sunday. Recently, some of Ferm's conclusions have been challenged by Cornelius Van Til. Van Til is an example of those orthodox Christians outside of fundamentalism who also frown upon cooperative evangelism.

Van Til is not convinced that Jesus' methods were those of cooperative evangelism. He points to Jesus' condemnation of the apostate religious teachers of His day. The Pharisees and Sadducees wanted nothing to do with Jesus' ministry. And so, Van Til tells us, "As they did not invite Jesus to cooperate in preaching *their* gospel with them so Jesus did not invite them to preach *his* gospel with him."[11]

While Van Til's argument at first seems valid, a more careful reading of it will reveal that it is based upon a false analogy. Naturally, the Pharisees did not invite Jesus to preach *their* gospel — Jesus would have refused! And naturally, Jesus did not invite the Pharisees to preach *His* Gospel — they would have refused! The proper analogy (and here there is no precedent in Jesus' ministry for Van Til to appeal to) would be found only if the Pharisees had asked Jesus to come and with their permission and cooperation still preach *His* Gospel! Evidently Van Til thinks that Jesus would have refused such an opportunity. I do not!

Van Til also refers to the conflict between Paul and the Judaizers as evidence that Paul would have frowned on cooperative evangelism. Van Til notes the bitter antipathy between Paul's preaching of grace and the Judaizers who preached salvation by ceremonial works. Between Paul and them, "It was a battle unto death. A church centered evangelism under the auspices of a committee, the membership of which was composed in part of the party of the Judaizers and in part of the party of Paul, would be all to the benefit of the Judaizers."[12]

No one can disagree with Van Til's remarks insofar as they apply to Paul. But is his analogy between the position

11Van Til. *op. cit.*, p. 26 (italics mine).
12*Ibid.*, p. 27.

of Paul and the situation in which the twentieth-century evangelist finds himself a proper one? If the situation in the church today is significantly different, then the analogy breaks down and Van Til is left without a scriptural objection to cooperative evangelism. We certainly do not wish to deny the similarity between the Judaizers and twentieth-century liberalism. Both represent autosoterism at its worst. But there *is* an important difference. In Paul's day, the Church was still relatively small and relatively pure of doctrinal error. The line between Christians and pagans was still clearly drawn. But today, in America, the people the evangelist wishes to reach for Christ are often nominally within the church. In other words, while they may be members of a particular church or consider themselves as belonging to one religious group or another, many are not committed Christians. In many cases, it is entirely correct to picture the American evangelist as outside the pale of professing Christendom attempting to find an audience within for his message. The question now boils down to the best method for reaching the mass of professing Christians who may yet be estranged from God because of sin. John W. Sanderson seems to have clearly seen the alternatives here when he speaks of "purity of testimony — or opportunity?"[13] But the evangelical believes that these are not exclusive disjuncts. Rather, he believes that it is possible to capitalize on the opportunities afforded by cooperative evangelism without sacrificing the purity of his message.

What message is Graham preaching? What message is it that liberals are sponsoring and that their church members are coming to hear? It is the old-fashioned Gospel of sin, judgment and salvation by grace. Graham believes that —

> The mission of the Church is to make the truth known, not just to preserve and protect it. Truth needs only to be proclaimed. But unless it is proclaimed to those whose need is greatest, the Church will have failed. It is for this reason that Billy Graham and his team have always accepted

[13]See John W. Sanderson, "Purity of Testimony — or Opportunity?" *Sunday School Times*, Feb. 11, 1961.

calls for leadership in evangelism, even though they realized that theological conformity can never be assured in
advance.[14]

Cornelius Van Til himself makes an interesting admission when he writes,

> Machen knew well enough that an *independent* board of
> missions was not a normal thing. He knew it was the task
> of the church to engage in evangelism and missions. But,
> when placed before the choice of a church-centered evan-
> gelism with modernism largely in control of the church
> or evangelism carried on by an independent board, he
> chose the latter.[15]

In other words, Van Til admits approvingly that
Machen recognized that in order effectively to perform the
task of evangelism and missions, one must sometimes do
things that a conservative would not *normally* do. Difficult
situations and demanding responsibilities call for desperate
action. And so the evangelical admits (or ought to admit)
that perhaps cooperative evangelism is not the *normal* thing.
But when faced with a choice between an evangelism that
reaches the masses and one that will not do it as effectively,
the evangelical chooses cooperative evangelism.

To set the record straight, we should make it clear that
while the separatists bemoan the "unscriptural" and "God-
dishonoring tactics" of Graham's methods, their own critical
attitudes and attacks against Graham betray these same
characteristics. These hyper-separatists[16] gloss over the fact
that Graham has not changed his Bible-centered message;
they gloss over the fruitful results of his campaigns. And in
place of this, they often offer distorted half-truths that are
frequently taken out of context.

There can be little doubt that this is one of the most
serious issues within orthodoxy. But regardless of who is
right, it is a sad testimony to an unbelieving world when

[14]Ferm, *op. cit.*, p. 22.
[15]Van Til, *op. cit.*, p. 28.
[16]It should be understood that we do not here have in mind such men as
Machen and Van Til. Van Til's protests are carried out on a high level of
scholarship and Christian courtesy. We are thinking instead of the more
radical right wing elements of orthodoxy, the "hyper-separatists," who care
little for the more basic elements of Christian charity or politeness.

Christians (and the participants in *this* dispute *are* committed Christians) cannot exhibit love toward one another. I believe that the following words by Robert Ferm are correct:

> Hence, the genuinely Christian disposition is not one of self-justification, but of love. Separatists have attempted to prove that they are right, but in their attempt they have neglected a far more important Christian virtue. Love is first in the list of the fruits of the spirit. It is the outgoing love of the redeemed personality which is the manifestation of the love of God shed abroad in the heart of the believer.[17]

Separatists should remember that there are, for the Christian, two kinds of heresy! There is first of all theological heresy, i.e., the departure from basic and central doctrines of the Bible and Christianity. But there is also a practical heresy which is a departure from *all* that God demands of us in our personal lives. Some fundamentalists have been so busy denouncing others of theological heresy that they have overlooked their own sins of the spirit. Their pride and lack of Christian love are in sharp contrast to the words of the One they call their Master — "By this shall all men know that ye are my disciples — *if ye love one another.*"

17Ferm, *op. cit.,* p. 92.

Part Four

EVANGELICALISM AND THE DEFENSE OF THE FAITH

Introduction to Part Four

EVANGELICALISM AND THE DEFENSE OF THE FAITH

Conservatives have been guilty of ignoring to a great extent the study of philosophy. They have often failed to recognize the philosophic assumptions underlying many of the criticisms against Christianity and have, therefore, in the eyes of many, failed to adequately defend their faith against these attacks. Evangelicals should be quick to show the elements and implications of Christian theism in as many areas of life as possible. H. B. Kuhn has put this well —

> A good case can be made for the contention that historic supernaturalism went into eclipse in the first quarter of the twentieth century, not because of any intrinsic deficiency in its message, but for lack of an adequate projection of that message into our national life. This lack of penetration of American thought by historic evangelicalism is not a simple phenomenon. In the first place, orthodoxy in America had not developed a definitive philosophic grounding.[1]

In the next two chapters, we shall attempt to examine the efforts of contemporary evangelicals to provide just such a philosophical grounding for orthodox Christianity.

[1]Harold B. Kuhn, "Philosophy of Religion," *Contemporary Evangelical Thought*, Great Neck, N. Y., Channel Press (c. 1957) p. 217.

CHAPTER 8

Philosophical Apologetics

As one would expect, many philosophical efforts by evangelicals are directed toward the defense of the Christian faith. Thus it is both rewarding and enlightening to notice some of the contemporary trends in the field of philosophical apologetics.

Since World War II, evangelicals have produced a number of significant scholarly works on apologetics. Carl Henry started the ball rolling in 1946 with his *Remaking the Modern Mind*. Carnell followed in 1948 with his *Introduction to Christian Apologetics* while Bernard Ramm entered the field with *Problems in Christian Apologetics* in 1949 and *Types of Apologetic System* in 1953. Gordon Clark's *Christian View of Men and Things* was published in 1952 and served a double purpose as an apology for Christianity and an introduction to philosophy. Cornelius Van Til[1] defended Christianity as well as himself in *The Defense of the Faith* (1955). Carnell's latest works on apologetics, *Christian Commitment* (1957) and *The Kingdom of Love and the Pride of Life* (1961), take a somewhat different approach from his earlier *Christian Apologetics*. Clark's *Thales to Dewey* (1957), although a history of philosophy (and it is being recognized as one of the best), is a remarkably subtle and effective argument for biblical theism. More recently, Clark has written another work dealing with various problems in the philosophy of religion, *Religion, Reason and Revelation* (1961).

This list of books is not by any means exhaustive, but

[1] While Van Til is not a neo-evangelical, his views on apologetics are similar enough to warrent his inclusion here.

it does represent the major efforts of these men who generally take a similar approach to the problems of philosophy and apologetics. An examination of the writings of these men reveals that their defense of Christianity is made on different grounds than that typified by the eighteenth and nineteenth-century approaches made by Butler, Paley and others. Perhaps the best name for this contemporary evangelical approach to apologetics is Presuppositionalism.

I. THE APOLOGETICS OF PRESUPPOSITIONALISM

A. *The Necessity of Basic Assumptions*

Every system of thought begins with certain presuppositions or assumptions. In fact, assumptions are necessary if we are to think at all. In the words of Augustine who saw this truth so long ago, we must believe something before we can know anything. Most people do not realize that whenever they think, there are some things that they assume, i.e., that they just take for granted. The consequences of these assumptions, for philosophy in general and for their thinking in particular, are most important.

As Gordon Clark puts it, "All thought depends on original assumptions. Just as the theorems of geometry are deduced from the axioms, so the conclusions of behaviorism are deduced from the assumption that mind is a physiological process."[2]

Often a beginning student of geometry tends to overlook the significance of the axioms at the beginning of his textbook. He rushes over them in order to get into the more important work of solving problems. The axioms, while basic to all the subsequent proofs, are themselves not proved, or even unprovable. However, the advanced student soon realizes that with regard to the ultimate validity of all subsequent argumentation, these basic axioms or presuppositions are much more important than all of the later problems and solutions. For the rest of the geometry follows only if the axioms are accepted. If they are denied, then the propositions originally deduced from the axioms

[2]Gordon Clark, *Christian View of Men and Things,* Grand Rapids, Eerdmans, 1951, p. 29.

do not follow (since there is now nothing for them to follow from) and the validity of the entire geometry is suspect.

In a similar way,[3] human knowledge depends on certain assumptions that are often unexpressed, sometimes unrecognized and frequently unproven.

B. The Nature of Basic Assumptions

As we have suggested, assumptions are basic to all knowledge and understanding. No one can know anything until he first believes (or assumes) something. Even the scientist makes certain epistemological, metaphysical and ethical assumptions. He assumes, for example, that knowledge is possible and sense experience is reliable, that the universe is regular and that scientists should be honest. Without these assumptions (which the scientist cannot justify within the limitations of his methodology), scientific inquiry would soon fail. These examples we have just given, however, are not, strictly speaking, *basic assumptions*. We might call them corollary assumptions since they are not the starting points of an argument and thus not directly connected with the investigation. The special concern of presuppositionalists is with the basic assumptions or presuppositions that are the logical starting points for metaphysical systems.

Basic assumptions are important because they determine the method and goal of theoretical thought.[4] Carnell compares them to a train running on tracks that have no switches. Once a man commits himself to a certain set of presuppositions, his direction and destination are determined. If, for example, a man begins with idealistic assumptions, he is logically committed (if consistent) to idealistic methods and conclusions. If he would change to pragmatism, he must first change his starting point. One's axioms always determine his theorems.

[3]We are not suggesting like the seventeenth-century Rationalists, Descartes and Spinoza, that all human knowledge is deductive. We recognize the fact of *a posteriori* knowledge but even this depends upon some things that are assumed.

[4]For a more thorough development of this thesis, see this writer's book, *Dooyeweerd and the Amsterdam Philosophy*, Grand Rapids, Zondervan, 1962.

The importance of absolutes, therefore, lies in their relation to faith or doubt. Once assumed, an absolute becomes the foundation for an order of thought, however simple or complex, which in turn elaborates a social and cultural pattern. Once doubted, the absolute may become the point of departure in the search for some other presupposition.[5]

In the strictest sense of the word, ultimate principles are incapable of proof, for they are either deduced from other premises or from themselves. If we deduce them from other premises, we have then proved them to be sure. The trouble is that they would then no longer be *basic* principles since the premises from which they were derived would be more ultimate. If, however, these principles are used in their own "proof," the supposed argument is then circular and not really a *proof* at all. Since there is no other alternative, it follows that basic assumptions cannot be proven. There is, however, a way in which they may be indirectly verified.

C. The Verification of Basic Assumptions

J. Oliver Buswell III has objected to presuppositionalist apologetics by writing:

> It will be appropriate at this point to call attention to a fallacy assumed in common by Dr. Clark and a considerable number of sincere Christian teachers of philosophy and theology in our generation. The fallacy is contained in the words in which Dr. Clark objects to anyone requiring a "proof of a first principle." Now it is true that when one begins a process of reasoning he must begin somewhere, he must make some assumptions, he must have some presuppositions. But the notion that presuppositions, or first principles, or initial assumptions, are not subject to questioning or re-examination is totally without support. . . . I totally repudiate the assumption that these foundations may not be questioned or re-examined or substantiated and reinforced.[6]

Buswell's objection rests on a total misunderstanding of the presuppositionalist position. Clark, Henry and Carnell are not pleading for any kind of irrationalism in religion or

5J. S. Boughton, "Concerning Moral Absolutes," *Journal of Philosophy*, LV, 1958, p. 311.
6J. Oliver Buswell III, "Review of Clark's *Christian View of Men and Things*," *Journal of the American Scientific Affiliation*, December, 1953, pp. 8, 9.

philosophy. On the contrary, they are urging that we conduct a rational and consistent investigation of the implications of every proposed basic assumption to see which assumptions are more probably true.

Perhaps since these men are, in a sense, "Neo-Augustinians," a brief reference to Augustine would help make their position clearer. Augustine often wrote of faith as an assumption or an hypothesis[7] that one accepts at the beginning of an investigation. But even though Augustine held that faith comes *before* reason in point of time, it was always with the qualification that faith bring us to a rational conclusion. We believe in order that we may know, wrote Augustine. He did not teach that faith does away with reason. On the contrary, reason supports faith. Bernard Ramm tells us that for Augustine,

> Constructive thought is possible only on a faith basis, viz, that we grant provisional status or truthfulness to propositions. A reason can only operate when interested and faith gives reason its interest and direction. But upon examination reason may then justly reject or accept what faith proposes . . . Faith is grounded, is tested, is verified, and verified testimony attains to a state of being free from doubt.[8]

But suppose, Gordon Clark asks, we are faced with a choice between two antithetic first principles. Which one shall we choose? Clark argues that we should choose the one which, when applied to the whole of reality, will give us the most coherent picture of the world. Clark believes that if tests for truth are applied throughout one's examination of a system, it will become evident which system is correct for "on this theory it would be impossible to have two self-consistent, mutually contradictory philosophies. A false statement, so it is said, will always, if pursued far enough, imply its own falsity."[9]

[7]The word, "faith," of course, has many meanings and uses. Here we are concerned only with what might be termed "philosophic faith" or what Carnell calls "general faith" (*Case*, p. 28) which is believing in a thing or proposition. "Vital Faith" is trusting in a person while the Christian concept of "saving faith" is a species of vital faith.

[8]Bernard Ramm, *Types of Apologetic Systems*, Wheaton, Ill., Van Kampen Press (c. 1953) p. 180.

[9]Clark, *op. cit.*, p. 30.

The method by which presuppositionalists seek to verify basic assumptions is neither new, original nor unique. The scientist uses a similar procedure in testing his hypothesis. The scientist's hypothesis is first tested by various experiments. If the hypothesis is consistent with the data uncovered by the experiments (assuming, of course, the accuracy and completeness of the experimentation), the hypothesis is considered to be verified and probably true. This account is over-simplified, of course, but it is sufficient for our present purpose.

Similarly, basic assumptions may be tested by following out their implications as they lead (logically) to a world view or metaphysical system. We then test the system for truth. If a world view can measure up to standards and tests for truth, it reflects reliability back upon its first principles.

The problem then is to discover criteria of truth by which we may test world views or metaphysical systems. Carnell talks about "systematic consistency" and Clark speaks of "coherence" as being the tests for truth. Their meaning is substantially the same. In this discussion, I prefer to follow the argument of Frederick Ferré (who acknowledges his indebtedness to Alfred North Whitehead). By this, I do not wish to suggest in any way that Ferré is sympathetic to the views of Clark and Carnell nor that I am a disciple of Whitehead. I have simply found that, in the matter of tests for truth, Ferré's argument closely parallels that of the presuppositionalists. I am referring to it because of what I judge to be its greater clarity.

Ferré is very aware of the prevailing philosophic sentiment against the possibility of verifying metaphysical systems. He notes that,

> Despite widespread negative answers to this question, I am increasingly coming around to the view that criteria can be found by which metaphysical systems can be graded . . . Is so far as metaphysical systems have a definite function, then, they can be judged according to their success in fulfilling this function.[10]

[10]Frederick Ferré, *Language, Logic and God*, Harper and Row, N. Y. (c. 1961) p. 162.

An adequate test for truth must take account of both rational (Ferré speaks of them as "internal") and empirical ("external") criteria. The rational criteria that any world view must satisfy are consistency and coherence. By consistency, we mean that the system must be free from internal self-contradictions. But as Ferré points out, "Consistency is obviously a negative criterion. Though any metaphysical system which can be convicted of an explicit self-contradiction deserves swift discard, few major metaphysical syntheses are easily vulnerable to this charge. Consistency is a necessary but not a sufficient condition for the acceptance of a metaphysical system."[11] By coherence, we mean that the various parts or principles of the system must stick together.

The empirical or external tests for truth are applicability and adequacy. Applicability means that the system must be relevant to experience, that is, the world view "must be capable of illuminating *some* experience naturally and without distortion."[12] Applicability means that this particular presupposition can better explain the available data more thoroughly than any other assumption. But even applicability is not enough for the system must also be adequate.

A conceptual synthesis must not only be applicable to some experience which it interprets; it must (much more demandingly) be adequate to *all* possible experience, if it is to succeed in being of unlimited generality; that is, it must show all experience to be interpreted without oversight, distortion or "explaining away" on the basis of its key concepts.[13]

Thus metaphysical systems must be and can be tested for truth on the basis of their consistency, coherence, applicability and adequacy.

But Clark then asks, what do we do if even after all our work we still find that there appear to be two more systems of thought that are more or less self-consistent? This situation might well develop since only someone with omniscience could apply the tests for truth with complete

11*Ibid.*
12*Ibid.*, p. 163.
13*Ibid.*

success. Clark states that in such a situation we must choose. We must choose that system which is more self-consistent, which more adequately satisfies all the tests for truth. In Clark's opinion, that system will be Christian theism. He admits that —

> the theistic view of the world faces difficulties. There are questions to which Christianity seems to give an inadequate answer or none at all. But does anyone claim that pragmatism or realism or idealism gives adequate answers to all questions? Is humanism or naturalism free of difficulty? There has been an immense amount, not merely of inadequacy but of inconsistency in some of the greatest philosophers . . . But if one system can provide plausible solutions to many problems while another leaves too many questions unanswered, if one system tends less to skepticism and gives more meaning to life, if one world view is consistent while others are self-contradictory, who can deny us, since we must choose, the right to choose the more promising first principle?[14]

Every world view, then, whether it be theistic or naturalistic, begins with certain basic assumptions. By testing these world views we may find out which presupposition, while still incapable of a strict demonstrative proof, provides the most promising basis for a world view. The Christian apologist insists on the absolute importance of beginning with the assumption of the existence of the God revealed in Scripture.

II. THE IMPLICATIONS OF PRESUPPOSITIONALISM

A. *The Importance of Starting with God and Revelation*

Presuppositionalists propose to begin by assuming (not proving) the existence of God and His revelation in the Bible. Carl Henry states the importance of this procedure:

> One must begin with God not only to get to God, but to get to anything. . . . From a certain vantage point, the concept of God is determinative for all other concepts; it is the Archimedean lever with which one can fashion an entire world view. If the great periods of philosophy have diversely interpreted history, the nature of man, and the

[14]Clark, *op. cit.*, p. 34.

space-time universe itself, these differences are traceable to variant presuppositions concerning God.[15]

If the reader feels that the presuppositionalist is begging the question, he is right! But the point that these men are trying to make is that everyone begs the question about the assumptions with which he starts his philosophy and there are no *prima facie* reasons why, at least in the beginning of an inquiry, the Christian assumption should be any worse than its denial.

Henry goes on to argue that —

> The modern attempts logically to prove the existence of the Christian God betray almost invariably a failure adequately to appreciate this revelatory principle. The Hebrew-Christian writers nowhere argue to God with Aristotle or any other philosopher as a stepping stone. And this not because of philosophic inability as much as an awareness of the significance of revelation. . . . Where God has spoken, revealed truth becomes the starting point of consistent knowledge; revelation is the test of truth, furnishes the framework and corrective for natural reason, introduces consistency into fragmentary human knowledge.[16]

Thus, the presuppositionalist position is that it is only on revelational ground that one can have a correct concept of God as the personal, soveregn, self-sufficient, omnipotent Creator and Judge of the universe.

B. The Knowledge of God and Natural Revelation

Many theologians have been confused about the presuppositionalist attitude toward natural revelation. Some critics of the position believe that presuppositionalism denies natural theology altogether. This is far from being the truth. What these men do argue is that sin has so affected man's reason that natural revelation is not sufficient to bring man to a knowledge of the Christian God.

Perhaps the presuppositionalist understanding of natural theology can be made clearer by comparing it to Immanuel Kant's theory of knowledge. Kant repudiated pure empiricism, i.e., the theory that knowledge could arise from sense

---

[15]Carl Henry, *Remaking the Modern Mind*, Grand Rapids, Eerdmans, (c. 1946) pp. 232, 171.
[16]*Ibid.*, pp. 196, 227.

perception alone. He argued instead that while knowledge originated in sense perception (i.e., our senses supplied data or precepts), the mind then had to act upon the mass of unorganized sense data in order to form concepts. In other words, the mind was able to arrive at knowledge only because it came to the world already equipped with a set of *a priori* categories by means of which it could interpret and organize the mass of data received through the senses. Without such an *a priori* structure of rationality, Kant argued, knowledge would be impossible.

Similarly, the presuppositionalist argues that apart from some kind of *a priori* knowledge of God in the soul, man would be unable to recognize God in His creation. The Christian believer sees evidence of God's existence in the creation only because he already knows about God. This *a priori* knowledge of God is a result of man's having been created in the image of God.

Carnell shows that this is the presuppositionalist position when he remarks, in commenting on Romans 1:20, that "Paul truly taught that God is known through sense perception but that does not involve us in empiricism. May it not equally be that, *knowing* God (by innate knowledge, which Paul teaches) we are *reminded* of Him in His works?"[17]

Carnell later locates the source of this innate knowledge in the image of God. This leads him to conclude that "Rather than building up a knowledge of God through a patient examination of the content of sense experience, we proceed to such experience *equipped* with an awareness of God."[18]

Presuppositionalists hold that the traditional arguments usually used in attempts to prove God's existence are invalid. Henry states that modern attempts to logically prove God's existence stem from the influence of Aquinas. Henry argues that this has led to an exclusion of the revelational principle and an acceptance of the Aristotelian philosophy

[17]E. J. Carnell, *Introduction to Christian Apologetics*, Grand Rapids, Eerdmans, 1948, p. 149n.
[18]*Ibid.*, p. 151n.

which is a necessary pre-requisite for Aquinas' so-called "five ways." Luther and Calvin, instead of following the lead of Aristotle and Aquinas, tried to recall the Church to base its faith in God's existence not on some inconclusive, invalid syllogism, but upon God's own self-disclosure in the Bible. But their pleas were forgotten as men became more and more enamored of the empirical arguments for the existence of God. Henry shows us that as Hume and Kant betrayed the weaknesses of the arguments, the adherents of these views still refused to return to revelation as the basis for the certainty of God's existence. Instead, Henry tells us, they traded certainty for probability or a "moral certainty" that God existed.

Van Til rejects both the traditional *a priori* and *a posteriori* proofs because, he feels, if the arguments prove the existence of any God, it is not the Christian God but only a finite deity. Clark, Henry and Carnell accept the Humian and Kantian criticisms of the traditional arguments. This does not mean that they are disciples of Hume or Kant but only that they believe that on this point Hume and Kant were correct. Presuppositionalists point to the one assumption which is common to all empirical approaches to the knowledge of God, namely, the belief that the cosmological, teleological and anthropological arguments all refer to the same deity. They agree that this conclusion goes beyond the empirical evidence, is pure assumption and cannot be shown to be so apart from special revelation.

Henry also states, "Hume has shown for all time, that empirically, one cannot get to the notion of an omnipotent, good god, but must take his choice between a god absolutely holy yet limited in power, or absolute in omnipotence but not wholly good."[19]

This facet of presuppositionalism has puzzled men. "Why," they ask, "should any Christian want to attack the traditional proofs?" There are at least two important reasons: (1) if an argument is fallacious (as the traditional

19Henry, *op. cit.*, p. 199f.

arguments are), it is utterly useless and intellectually dishonest to use it regardless of how important the thing is that one may be trying to prove;[20] (2) presuppositionalists are trying, as did the Reformers, to call the Christian Church back to the utter and absolute importance of God's self-revelation of Himself in Scripture. The proper starting point for any adequate theology must be special revelation.

C. The Problem of Common Ground

One of the most important and difficult issues raised by the presuppositionalists is that over the existence of common ground between Christian and non-christian systems of thought, between believers and unbelievers. To be sure, it is not a new issue but recent controversies over the matter have been stirred up by the writings of Van Til and Clark. This is one matter on which there is more than a little disagreement among presuppositionalists. In fact, it provides perhaps the biggest gap between the position of Van Til and that of other presuppositionalists.

Van Til believes that it is impossible to separate a fact from its ultimate interpretation. Therefore, a non-Christian always interprets facts according to non-Christian categories of thought that make, not God, but man the ultimate point of reference. The Christian makes not himself but God the ultimate reference point and thus always interprets facts according to divine categories of thought. In other words, facts are not only God-created but for the Christian they must be God-interpreted as well.

Gordon Clark finds not only ambiguity but also some inconsistency in Van Til's argument. Clark believes that Van Til "denies true knowledge to the unregenerate. As a matter of fact, he (Van Til) goes further and implies that no human being can have knowledge."[21] Clark rejects Van

[20]Many forget, at this juncture, that the invalidity of an argument does not imply anything about the falsity of its conclusion. Logical validity and truth are two entirely different matters. Thus, the invalidity of the theistic proofs implies nothing about the truth or falsity of the proposition, "God exists."

[21]Gordon Clark, "Apologetics," in Contemporary Evangelical Thought, op. cit., p. 159.

Til's apparent position as being not only contrary to the views of Calvin and Scripture but also as leading to skepticism.

Clark, differing with Van Til, holds that while there may be no common ground on the level of *systems,* there may be on the level of *persons.*[22] Clark disagrees with Van Til's apparent assertion that an unregenerate man can have no true knowledge. He states that due to the noetic effects of sin, "perhaps the human consciousness is not always able to overcome sluggishness and correct mistakes in reasoning. The point I wish to insist on is that this is sometimes possible. An unregenerate man can know some true propositions and can sometimes reason correctly."[23] Thus, while there is no common ground between the Christian faith and, for example, naturalism, there may be and must be some point of contact between a Christian and a naturalist. Otherwise, any communication between the two would be impossible.

D. Presuppositionalists on the Attack

Evangelicals have learned to use the principles of presuppositionalism as a tool in criticizing contending systems of philosophy and theology. One such system is religious modernism. Henry has attacked this movement in two books, *Remaking the Modern Mind* and *The Drift of Western Thought.* In the former,

> He traces the manner in which the major presuppositions of the "modern man" have been challenged, and even undermined, by the events of the twentieth century and indicates that the net result is an *impasse.*[24]

With his gods dead, with his presuppositions undermined, where can the modern man turn? Henry shows that modern man has been conditioned against a return to the

22See Clark, "Apologetics," pp. 155f and Carnell, *Christian Apologetics,* pp. 212ff.
23Gordon Clark, "The Bible as Truth," *Bibliotheca Sacra,* April, 1957, pp. 161f.
24Harold B. Kuhn, "Philosophy of Religion," *Contemporary Evangelical Thought, op. cit.,* p. 244.

foundations of Western civilization, that is, to the assumptions of Christianity. Henry argues that a "recovery from the frustration and pessimism which mark modern man's present mood must be preceded by a recapture of certain controlling ideas. In other words, there must be restored to both philosophy and science 'a revelational context.'"[25] The assumptions which Henry challenges include the inevitability of human progress, the inherent good of man, the ultimate reality of nature and the ultimate animality of man.

> Harold Kuhn comments,
> This volume is highly significant in terms of its survey of the role of Christian presuppositions — the principle of Christian philosophy, if you will — in human culture. . . . In his *Drift of Western Thought*, Henry . . . traces the cultural impact of the reception or abandonment of the Christian world view, showing the final alternatives to be: Christian supernaturalism or thoroughgoing naturalism. . . . Henry makes it clear that the real *issue* is one of "starting points" or presuppositions, and shows that between the presuppositions of historic evangelicalsm and those of the classic liberalism were differences of the most profound sort.[26]

Presuppositionists have also challenged the assumptions of Neo-Thomism, the twentieth century revival of Thomas Aquinas' synthesis of Christianity and Aristotelianism. Henry disagrees with Thomism because it begins with neotheistic premises. He argues that the same evidence which is so convincing to every Thomist does not lead every nontheist to theistic conclusions. "There is more significance than usually thought in the statement that only a Christian could have dreamed the 'five fold proof' (of Aquinas)."[27] Henry believes that Thomism is destined to failure because natural theology contains presuppositions which rule out a Christian philosophy. He urges that before revelational truth can be defended against contemporary criticisms, the

[25]*Ibid.*
[26]*Ibid.*
[27]Henry, *Remaking the Modern Mind, op. cit.,* p. 225.

presuppositions of natural theology must be disputed. Henry's view warns against any misuse of philosophy that excludes the possibility of God's existence in its very presuppositions.

Finally, presuppositionalists have laid bare the role that faith plays, even in modern scientific naturalism. Henry writes that even the scientist who denies supernaturalism and religious faith cannot himself —

> . . . operate without faith. Science continually works within undemonstrable postulates; without them the scientific enterprise would collapse. At point after point, the scientist *believes* in order to *know*. He believes in the continuity of personal identity; in the evidence of his sense; in the reliability of the laws of thought; in the value of honesty in research; in the dependability of the laws he charts. These beliefs make demonstration possible, yet they are not demonstrable beliefs.[28]

Henry makes it quite plain that he is not advocating that

> . . . modern science be disclaimed — not by any means. But the assumptions that modern science has mediated to us, the subtle network of unproved dogmas rooted in the prejudices of the modern mind rather than in the demands of reality upon us — these are the premises which must be patiently sifted out. It is in the name of science that the modern man was taught inevitable progress, essential goodness, natural ultimacy, and man's animality — and now we need to take away all doubt that the name of science was blasphemed by false prophets . . . So authoritative and deep-rooted was the modern scientific naturalism, despite a three-century infancy in the history of philosophy, that the university minds who most ridiculed the authority of the Scriptures seemed hardly to suspect that they had substituted one authority for another.[29]

Thus presuppositionalism is both a negative and positive approach to philosophical apologetics. It is a negative criticism of non-Christian and quasi-Christian systems of thought. In a sense, it is attempting to "demythologize" the thought of modern man, that is, unmask the prejudices that

[28]Carl Henry, "Science and Religion" in *Contemporary Evangelical Thought, op. cit.,* p. 262.
[29]Henry, *Modern Mind, op. cit.,* p. 266f.

have made him reject biblical theism as well as point out the inadequacies of his substitute for Christianity. But presuppositionalism is also a positive attempt to put forth a distinctive defense and exposition of biblical theism as well as an explanation of its implications for every area of life.

Presuppositionalism and Its Critics

Presuppositionalism and Its Critics

Presuppositionalism has been the victim of many misunderstandings and much misguided criticism. In this chapter we shall look at the most important of these objections. Our purpose is not only to show the irrelevance or invalidity of the arguments, but also, by contrasting presuppositionalism with the many misunderstandings of it, develop and explain the position more fully.

I. WHAT ABOUT THE EPISTEMOLOGICAL STARTING POINT?

In his book, *The Resurrection of Theism*, Stuart Hackett has presented several criticisms of presuppositionalism. His major objection seems to be directed against the presuppositionalist claim that basic assumptions are metaphysical in nature. In opposition, Hackett's procedure "involves, not the assumption of a metaphysical starting-point, but the assumption of an epistemological ground, common to all rational beings, in terms of which the adequacy of any speculative doctrine may be tested with something approaching final authority."[1] Hackett then defines what he means by an epistemological starting point. "We assume, in such an approach, a universal structure of rationality, both in the mind and in the real world — such a structure in fact, as we have defended in our espousal of rational empiricism."[2] Thus, Hackett agrees with the presuppositionalist that everyone begins with certain assumptions. But these

[1]Stuart Hackett, *The Resurrection of Theism*, Chicago, Moody Press, (c. 1957) p. 155.
[2]*Ibid.*

assumptions, he insists, are not metaphysical in nature but epistemological. He argues, "Of course, there is a starting point, but it is not the assumption of the first reality: it is rather the epistemological starting-point of rational empiricism."[3]

Hackett's discussion is much too long and involved to present in detail. But we believe that we can lay our finger on the basic snare in his argument quite quickly. Our evaluation of his argument against the priority of the metaphysical assumptions (the position of Clark and Carnell) and for the priority of his own epistemological starting-point will be based on our claim that Hackett has misread his opponents. If we can show that he has not understood presuppositionalism, then it seems quite clear that his arguments and criticism will have little relevance.

Hackett seems bothered by the presuppositionalist claim that the metaphysical starting point determines the methods and conclusions of the rest of the system. He believes that Carnell holds that the metaphysical presupposition determines even certain aspects of epistemology which Hackett thinks must come before any metaphysical ultimate is chosen. Hackett quotes Carnell to the effect that "A man's attitude to what he considers to be the highest logical ultimate in reality determines the validity of his synoptic starting point, his method and his conclusions. The Christian . . . (has) chosen as his logical starting point the existence of the God who has revealed Himself in Scripture."[4] Hackett then *interprets* Carnell to mean: Carnell's "synoptic starting point equals epistemological starting point in my parlance."[5] This last statement reveals the mistake that undergirds the whole of Hackett's confused objection. On the basis of his identification of his *epistemological* starting point with Carnell's *synoptic* starting point, Hackett understands Carnell to mean that the "Basic meta-

[3]*Ibid.*
[4]Edward John Carnell, *Introduction to Christian Apologetics*, Grand Rapids, Eerdmans, 1948, p. 212.
[5]Hackett, *op. cit.*, p. 159n.

physical postulate determines the validity of the epistemological starting point."[6]

In order to support our contention that Hackett has misunderstood Carnell (and presuppositionalism), let us look more closely at what Carnell has to say about starting points. On pages 124 ff. of his *Introduction to Christian Apologetics*, Carnell distinguishes between three different possible starting points: the temporal, logical and synoptic. The temporal starting point is irrelevant to our present discussion so we may ignore it. Carnell defines his logical starting point as "what one logically conceives as the over-all synthesizing element which unites the particulars" of the space-time universe.[7] Carnell's logical starting point, then, is equivalent to what has previously been termed the metaphysical ultimate or starting point. Carnell's synoptic starting point is that "which, when carried out to the end, will establish the grounds for what the system requires as its logical starting point."[8] In other words, a synoptic starting point is relative since it is chosen according to how well it aids one in proving his metaphysical (or logical) starting point. Carnell's synoptic starting point, then, is not a rational structure common to the minds of all men (as Hackett claims), but simply the point of experience from which a man believes he can best proceed to prove his first metaphysical principle (or logical starting point). Thus, Hackett is clearly wrong in his attempt to identify his epistemological starting point with Carnell's synoptic starting point.

But let us go one step further. It is this writer's contention that Carnell, Clark and the rest *do* presuppose what might be termed a common rationality of men. Clark has made several remarks that confirm this belief and which serve to support our claim that Hackett has made a serious blunder. Clark wrote in the last chapter of *A Christian View of Men and Things*:

6*Ibid.*, p. 167.
7Carnell, *op. cit.*, p. 124.
8*Ibid.*, p. 125.

Throughout the chapters of this volume certain presuppositions relative to the possibility, the nature, and the methods of knowledge have appeared beneath an historical, scientific, or religious surface. . . . Even systems of philosophy, like Neoscholasticism, which make metaphysics and being rather than epistemology and knowing the logical basis of their theory, must still meet the most serious objection to their views in the field of epistemology. The question, how do you know may sound simple enough; but the answer *virtually controls the whole system of philosophy.*[9]

Or consider the following:

If the arguments of the past few paragraphs are sound, along with the considerations on empiricism that occured in several of the earlier chapter, a satisfactory theory of epistemology must be some sort of a *priorism* (Hackett's "rational empiricism" is an *a priori* theory of knowledge) with or without intellectual intuition. The notion that a blank mind can learn must be repudiated. Of all the modern philosophers, it is Immanuel Kant who is naturally thought of first as a representative of *a priori* theory.[10]

A quick glance through the early pages of Hackett's *Resurrection of Theism* wll reveal his great indebtedness to the epistemology of Kant.

It seems clear, then, that presuppositionalists as well as Hackett recognize some sort of *a priori* rationality (in the form of a categorical structure) in men and admit that men possess this structure of rationality before they can choose a metaphysical ultimate. But since the categorical structure of rationality is common to all men (by virtue of their possession of the image of God) and the metaphysical assumptions underlying their world views are not, it seems that the best place to begin the argument is with the metaphysical ultimate.

II. THE PROBLEM OF COMMON GROUND

J. Oliver Buswell, Jr. has criticized presuppositionalism in his book, *A Christian View of Being and Knowing.* Most of Buswell's remarks in this connection are quite obscure because he has insisted on letting his opponents remain

---

[9]Gordon Clark, *Christian View of Men and Things,* Grand Rapids, Eerdmens, 1951, p. 285 (italics mine).
[10]*Ibid.,* p. 312.

anonymous which makes it exceedingly difficult to check on the accuracy of his statements. At times one receives a rather strong impression that Buswell's ambiguity only obscures what would otherwise be clearly seen to be false. For example, he tells us, "Influential Christian scholars in our generation are teaching that since man exists in a fallen condition, and since his mind is distorted by sin, there is no common ground, in reason or in evidences, between the Christian and his message, on the one hand, and the unbeliever on the other. This view (sic) has been called 'presuppositionalism' . . . "[11] However, we have already shown that with but one exception, presuppositionalists (Clark, Henry and Carnell) explicitly state that there is a realm of common ground. The only man whom Buswell's sweeping generalization might apply to would be Cornelius Van Til.

Stuart Hackett does a similar injustice to the position. He criticizes the views of both Van Til and Carnell,[12] but the significant thing is that he entirely ignores the position of Gordon Clark who holds that there is common ground on the level of persons. Clark himself has criticized Van Til and, for that matter, Carnell as well.[13] However, his criticism of Carnell is based not on Carnell's denial of common ground but on some confusions and apparent inconsistencies in his argument.

Clark (and to a lesser extent, Carnell) has shown that a denial of common ground between the believer and the unbeliever is not a necessary facet of presuppositionalism. Thus, any objection to presuppositionalism as a whole which is based on its supposed denial of common ground commits the fallacy of composition. This fallacy is committed whenever anyone argues that since something is true of the parts of any class, it is therefore true of the whole class. One might just as well argue that since Van Til and Carnell have blue eyes that, therefore, *all* presuppositionalists have blue eyes.

11J. Oliver Buswell, Jr., *A Christian View of Being and Knowing*, Grand Rapids, Zondervan, (c. 1960) p. 176.
12See Hackett, *op. cit.*, p. 170f.
13See Clark, "Apologetics" in *Contemporary Evangelical Thought*, Great Neck, N. Y., Channel Press. (c. 1957) pp. 154ff.

III. A LOGICAL FALLACY?

Presuppositionalists urge that the proper method for the Christian apologist is to begin by first assuming (and not proving) the existence of God and then testing the world view implied by this assumption by means of criteria for truth. It is claimed that this procedure will justify the assumption that God exists.

However, it might occur to some (although this writer has never yet seen this objection in print) that this whole procedure is fallacious and, in fact, commits the fallacy of affirming the consequent. A brief detour into logic will help make this clear.

A mixed hypothetical syllogism is an argument containing a hypothetical statement (such as, "If Rockefeller lives in Albany, then he lives in New York State"), a categorical statement (such as, "Rockefeller lives in New York"), and a conclusion drawn from these two premises. The only valid forms of this type of argumentation are found when either the antecedent of the hypothetical statement is affirmed or the consequent is denied. For example:

> If Rockefeller lives in Albany, then he lives in New York State.
> Rockefeller lives in Albany (the antecedent is affirmed).
> Therefore: Rockefeller lives in New York State.

The above is a valid argument as is the following:

> If Rockefeller lives in Albany, then he lives in New York State.
> Rockefeller does *not* live in New York State (denying consequent).
> Therefore: Rockefeller does *not* live in Albany.

However, one fallacy of this type of reasoning is committed by first affirming the consequent and then affirming the antecedent in the conclusion. The invalidity of this procedure is clearly seen in the following example:

> If Rockefeller lives in Albany, then he lives in New York State.
> He lives in New York State (affirming the consequent).
> Therefore: Rockefeller lives in Albany.

In this last example the conclusion does not follow. Simply because a man lives in New York State is not sufficient ground to conclude that he therefore lives in Albany.

Does the presuppositionalist commit this fallacy? He certainly seems to. If he does, how can the presuppositionalist possibly hope to salvage his theory in the face of what appears to be an obvious logical fallacy?

In chapter 8 we suggested that there was a decided similarity between the methodology of the presuppositionalist and that found in the area of the natural sciences. For example, a scientist often reasons as follows:

> If my hypothesis is true, then certain facts will be observable.
> Those facts are observable (via experimentation).
> Therefore: my hypothesis is true.

This procedure is used to justify the scientist's hypothesis, but it does so only by apparently breaking the laws of the hypothetical syllogism, in this case, by affirming the consequent.

Lewis Beck in his book, *Philosophic Inquiry*, has attempted to deal with this problem as it exists for the scientist. He writes, "We must conclude either that such scientific work is based on a logical fallacy, or that scientific verification is somewhat different from what it appears to be on the surface. Fortunately, the latter is the case."[14]

I am interested in seeing if Beck succeeds in his attempt to rescue scientific verification from the pit of this logical fallacy as well as discovering if his argument may possibly be applied to the problem of verification as it exists for the presuppositionalist. The following discussion, of necessity, decidedly simplifies Beck's argument.

Beck shows that the first step in scientific verification is, indeed, an example of affirming the consequent. Letting "H_1" stand for the first hypothesis to be tested and "F" stand for the facts or data or results of experiments set up to test the hypothesis, we get the following:

14Lewis White Beck, *Philosophic Inquiry: An Introduction to Philosophy.* © 1952, Prentice-Hall, Inc., Englewood Cliffs, N. J. Used by permission.

If H_1 is true, then F will be observable.
F is observable.
Therefore: H_1 is true.

The trouble with all this is that as long as our experimental procedure affirms the consequent, we cannot be sure that the data we have is not consistent with some other hypothesis (H_2, H_3, . . . H_n) which in fact might even explain the "facts" better.

Thus, we must find some way of eliminating the rival hypotheses that might possibly explain our present data. The scientist does this by submitting the rival hypothesis to a "crucial experiment." This will produce some observably different results and enable him to determine which hypothesis is more probably true. The situation now is something like this:

If H_1 is true, then F should be observable.
F is observable.
Therefore: H_1 is true.

By itself, the above procedure (as we have already noted) is fallacious and, at best, H_1 may be said to be only tentatively true. But, Beck argues, when the above procedure is taken *in conjunction with* the following step, the fallacy is avoided.

If H_2 (a rival hypothesis) is true, then F should be observable.[15]
F is not observable.
Therefore: H_2 is not true.

To be sure, the scientist has affirmed the consequent of H_1. But by means of the crucial experiment, he has denied the consequent of H_2 (a valid procedure) which gives him sufficient logical ground for saying that H_2 is refuted. And as Beck adds, "If H_2 is the only alternative to H_1 . . . this is sufficient logical ground for saying that H_1 is true."[16]

In other words, we posit a disjunctive syllogism in which either H_1 or H_2 is true. The scientist then shows by means of a crucial experiment that H_2 is false, thereby proving that H_1 is true.[17]

[15] i.e., as a result of our "crucial experiment."
[16] *Ibid.*, p. 97.
[17] For those familiar with logic: H_1 or H_2, not H_2, Therefore: H_1.

However, there is one more difficulty. Since we can never be certain that H_2 is the only alternative to H_1, the most we can say (speaking again in terms of logical certainty and not moral certainty) is that in the light of available evidence, there is no rival hypothesis which cannot be refuted, and thus we recognize H_1 as true.

Beck sums up his argument by stating,

> We must, to be sure, show that it (the hypothesis we are considering) does pass all the tests we put it to, and evidence of widely divergent kinds ought to converge upon it. But we must also show that the other hypotheses do *not* pass all the tests we put to them. Convergence of evidence . . . and elimination of alternatives, therefore, are the two prerequisites for accepting a hypothesis as true.[18]

Now let us return to our original question: does the presuppositionalist commit the fallacy of affirming the consequent? Let us review what we noticed in our last chapter about the verification of basic assumptions. First, we suggested that the implications of any basic assumption must be tested for truth. These tests for truth, of necessity, go beyond the observational tests of the scientist. They include consistency, coherence, applicability and adequacy. Beck has argued that scientific hypotheses must pass specific (albeit, "observational") tests. So, too, the presuppositionalist insists that we test the truth of our basic assumptions.

Secondly, we referred to Gordon Clark's argument that when we are faced with two antithetic first principles (rival hypotheses?), we must choose the one which, when applied to the whole of reality, gives the most coherent picture of reality. In other words, Clark's second step is the elimination of rival assumptions by showing that they do *not* meet all the tests for truth.

I admit that the above argument is simplified and that, perhaps, much more needs to be written about it. But for the present, I conclude: if scientific verification avoids the fallacy in question in the way suggested by Beck (and his argument seems sound), then presuppositionalism (since

[18]*Ibid.*, p. 98.

it clearly follows a similar procedure) also avoids the fallacy of affirming the consequent.

IV. BY WHAT STANDARD?

Although Cornelius Van Til is a presuppositionalist, he wants it understood that on several significant issues he disagrees with Clark and Carnell. The heart of his objection is implied by the title of a recent book explaining his thought, *By What Standard?*

Van Til complains that Clark and company only pay "lip service" to the presupposition of God and the Scriptures. He claims that Clark really begins by presupposing "laws" (such as the law of contradiction) and "facts." The assertion that Clark appeals to "facts" is a misrepresentation of his (although not of Carnell's) position and may be dismissed without further consideration. Clark has stated quite clearly, both in his *Christian View of Men and Things* and in his article on "Apologetics" in *Contemporary Evangelical Thought,* that "The English word *fact* has too many connotations to be useful in a carefully formulated theory."[19] However, Van Til's first objection, namely, that Clark and Carnell appeal to "laws" such as the law of contradiction, deserves further consideration.

Rousas Rushdoony clarifies this objection by writing that Clark and Carnell "reason from man's principle to God and enthrone our law (i.e., the law of contradiction) over God as basic to all human and divine processes."[20] Notice that for Rushdoony (as well as for Van Til), the law of contradiction as used by Clark is an arbitrary human law. Rushdoony adds, "If the law or principle is the basic tool for understanding, then it and not God is basic to thinking, to interpretation."[21] Again he tells us,

> Rationalism sought to interpret reality in terms of certain a priori principles. These a priori principles, however, were not anchored in the ontological trinity or in eternity but in the human mind as ultimate. . . . Can man, as Carnell

[19]Clark, "Apologetics," *op. cit.,* p. 145.
[20]Rousas J. Rushdoony, *By What Standard?,* Philadelphia, Presbyterian and Reformed Publishing Co., 1959, p. 22.
[21]*Ibid.,* p. 22f.

seems sometimes to argue, establish laws of logical or moral contradiction and hold whatever gods may be to meeting them, or must man meet God's standard?[22]

The objection of Van Til and Rushdoony is thus clear. Man is confronted with an "either-or" situation. The ultimate standard is either some man-made criterion (whatever this means) such as the law of contradiction, or else it is God! However, Van Til and Rushdoony seem not to realize that there is a way out of this dilemma. Van Til has posited a disjunction to which there is another valid, and consistently Christian, alternative. Van Til constantly speaks of the law of contradiction (at least, as it is found in Clark's philosophy) as if it were a human law. But what if it is a divine law, i.e., a God-created law? And in fact, what if the law of contradiction can be shown to be not only a divine law of thought but first and foremost a divine law of being? Clark asserts the following propositions:

(1) The law of contradiction is primarily a law of being, that is, it has ontological status. In *Thales to Dewey,* Clark discusses Aristotle's views concerning the law of contradiction. There is space here to note little more than Clark's conclusions. He argues that the principle of contradiction —

> . . . is stated not merely as a law of thought, but primarily as a law of being. The ontological form is basic, the purely logical is derivative: it becomes a law of thought because it is first a law of being.[23]

(2) The law of contradiction is indispensable to significant speech and action. Again, Clark's arguments are too involved to reproduce here so we shall notice only his conclusion. Besides, we are primarily interested in seeing if Van Til's argument is valid. Clark's point here is, to put it briefly, that a denial of the principles of logic leads only to skepticism.

> If contradictory statements are true of the same subject at the same time, evidently all things will be the same thing. Socrates will be a ship, a house, as well as a man; but then

22*Ibid.,* pp. 44, 81.
23Gordon Clark, *Thales to Dewey,* Boston, Houghton-Mifflin Co., (c. 1957) p. 98.

Crito too will be a ship, a house, and a man. But if precisely the same attributes attach to Crito that attach to Socrates, it follows that Socrates is Crito. . . . In fact, everything will be everything. Therefore everything will be the same thing. All differences among things will vanish and all will be one. *Such is the metaphysical nonsense to be derived from Protagoras or anyone else* (Van Til?) *who denies the law of contradiction.*[24]

When the law of contradiction is denied, a word can then mean both itself and its opposite. But when words can have contradictory meanings, they have no meaning and the result is pure nonsense. Meaning depends upon a word meaning one thing at a time. When this is not the case (and it is certainly not the case when the law of contradiction is denied), knowledge becomes impossible and the result is skepticism.

(3) The law of contradiction is not a man-made law (whatever that could mean in this connection) nor a law which man elevates over God. Rather, it is a God-decreed and God-given law. I am well aware that such expressions as these are viewed with suspicion by Positivists and Analytical philosophers. But this is hardly the place to make a detour into how I would propose to verify these statements or analyze their peculiar function. It shall have to suffice here to simply say that within the context of Christian theology, these expressions do have meaning for Christian philosophers and theologians. Returning to our discussion, we find that Clark deals with the problem of how man, even sinful man, can know the law of contradiction. He suggests that the categories of man's understanding —

> . . . are neither innate . . . nor derived from experience, but are merely subjective aptitudes for thought implanted in us contemporaneously with our existence, which were so ordered and disposed by our Creator that their exercise perfectly harmonizes with the laws of nature which regulate experience.[25]

Clark reminds us that Immanuel Kant had objected to this possibility but Clark examines his arguments and finds

[24]*Ibid.*, p. 103 (italics mine).
[25]Clark, *Christian View, op. cit.*, p. 314.

them deficient.[26] Clark further points out that Kant never did succeed in providing an adequate explanation of the fact that the same categories are possessed in common by all men. He asks,

> What hypothesis provides a ground for the common pos-
> session of the categories as adequately as Christian theism
> does? Though the existence and nature of God is in-
> susceptible of formal demonstration, yet if Christian theism
> is true, there is no mystery in the fact that all human minds
> use the same categories . . . Skepticism is ruled out and
> truth becomes possible.[27]

Thus Van Til's claim that Clark's presuppositionalism betrays the Christian cause by elevating a man-made law above God is confused and not to the point. The Christian, in using logic to test for truth, only honors a God-created law that is basic to all significant speech and knowledge.

The following remarks by Carnell provide a fitting rebuttal to all who would apparently divorce Christian theism from the canons of reason and logic:

> No man can meaningfully deny the primacy of the laws
> of logic. Their universality and necessity are secured by
> the simple fact that nothing has significance apart from
> them. Men do not invent the fundamental laws of logic,
> for nothing would mean anything if logic did not first
> mean what it says. . . . Even the man who tries to argue
> against the priority of logic must in his argument employ the
> very canons which he is seeking to destroy. Using logic
> to disprove logic is as foolish as catching rapid breaths
> while preaching that it is not necessary to breathe.[28]

V. CONCLUSION

In this chapter we have attempted to examine some of the objections already raised to the presuppositionalist's defense of the faith. We believe these arguments must be found wanting because, in almost every instance, their apparent plausibility rests upon a misunderstanding or misrepresentation of the presuppositionalist approach to apologetics.

[26]*Ibid.*, pp. 314ff.
[27]*Ibid.*, p. 318.
[28]Edward John Carnell, *Philosophy of the Christian Religion*, Grand Rapids, Eerdmans, 1952, p. 184.

Part Five

EVANGELICALISM AND ITS CRITICS

Introduction to Part Five

EVANGELICALISM AND ITS CRITICS

Evangelicalism is not without its critics. It is not our purpose here to examine the objections raised by those outside of Protestant orthodoxy. Their hostility toward a Gospel of grace, a divine Savior and an inspired Word continues unabated against all (whether they be called evangelicals or fundamentalists) who hold to these beliefs. What does concern us is the measure of protest coming from within conservative Protestantism.

While the nature of our study in the next two chapters will require our remarks to be at times somewhat pointed, our words are not intended as a personal attack against any of the men with whose views we shall be forced to disagree. They are brethren in Christ and we honor them as such. However, since we are disagreeing with what we believe are serious errors, we have not hesitated to be as clear or as blunt as we have to be.

Evangelicals: The Half-hearted Heretics?

Conservative critics of evangelicalism are divided into two camps. There are, on the one hand, those who believe that evangelicals are sincere but misguided brethren. The critics of this persuasion claim that evangelicals are mistaken in their methods, in some of their beliefs, and in some of their criticisms of fundamentalism. Those who regard evangelicalism in this light are much concerned lest some of these errors eventually lead evangelicals away from orthodoxy. As Robert Lightner puts it, "Has the product been changed with the changing of the wrapping? . . . Will the new label provide the opportunity for a different product in the future?"[1] The other group of critics is convinced that evangelicals are, in a way, half-hearted heretics, i.e., they have already departed from the faith of their fathers in many important respects. In this chapter we shall look at some of the claims made by this latter group. We believe that the previous arguments of this book will enable us to dismiss most of them quite quickly.

I. ARE EVANGELICALS COMPROMISING THE FAITH?

Rev. William Ashbrook has called evangelicalism "The New Neutralism." Many fundamentalists share his belief that evangelicals are compromising on matters essential to orthodoxy. Ashbrook warns,

Bible-believing Christians would do well to beware of this New Neutralism for four valid reasons. First, it is a movement born of compromise. Second, it is a movement

[1]Robert Lightner, *Neo-Evangelicalism*, Dunham Publishing Co., Findlay, Ohio, 1962, p. 36.

nurtured on pride of intellect. Third, it is a movement growing on appeasement of evil. And finally, it is a movement doomed by the judgment of God's Holy Word.[2]

Mr. Ashbrook's argument is regrettable, for while his accusations are vaguely formulated, unclearly supported and decidedly misleading, they will nonetheless succeed in confusing many uninformed Christians. Let us consider his claims in order.

A. Was Evangelicalism Born of Compromise?

In the second chapter of this book we offered sufficient documented proof from the early writings of the evangelicals that there was no thought of compromise behind their actions. The new evangelicalism arose to fill the spiritual and intellectual vacuum created by fundamentalism's forfeiture of its task in many areas. To accuse these men of compromise can only be due to a petty and biased misreading of history.

B. Is Evangelicalism a Movement Nurtured on Pride of Intellect?

Again in chapter 2 we made reference to the tendency toward anti-intellectualism that has become so characteristic of some segments of fundamentalism. It is difficult to see how Ashbrook's objection (which has recently been echoed by Lightner[3]) does anything but support our earlier claim. The evangelical desires to study philosophy and science so that he might defend the Christian faith from attacks made in the names of these false idols — is this pride of intellect? The evangelical believes that the most important task in the world (the propagation and defense of the Gospel) requires the best possible preparation — is this pride of intellect? The evangelical pleads for more dedicated Christians who are trained in the arts and sciences and who can show the relevance of the Christian message for their respective areas of specialization — is this pride of intellect? The word that

[2]William A. Ashbrook, "The New Evangelicalism — The New Neutralism," *Central Conservative Baptist Quarterly*, Summer, 1959.
[3]Lightner, *op. cit.*, p. 121ff.

most quickly comes to mind as descriptive of this position is "anti-intellectualism."

C. Is Evangelicalism a Movement Growing on the Appeasement of Evil?

Ashbrook is only one of a large company of fundamentalists who have made this charge. However, this accusation is somewhat ambiguous because it can mean two entirely different things.

First, the opponents of evangelicalism who say this may be thinking of evangelical attempts to carry on a dialogue with those of different theological persuasion. If evangelicals tended to ignore the differences between historic Protestant orthodoxy and such movements as neo-orthodoxy, then the charge might be justified. But Henry, Ramm, Clark and the others have continued unceasingly to mark off the differences between their theology and other positions unsympathetic to a biblical theology.

On the other hand, those who say this may believe that evangelicalism is fostering worldliness in the church. They may have in mind such statements as the following one by Carl Henry:

> Certain actions may be condemned for inadequate reasons, and the discerning Christian is called upon to protest. The Fundamentalist attitude toward dancing, movies and wine often takes an extreme form. These are by nature evil, some say; they are always and everywhere to be resisted. This attitude is "word-renouncing" in its presuppositions. It wrongly regards as intrinsically evil that which is in fact not so. . . . There is nothing intrinsically evil about the camera or dancing or wine.[4]

Now if this is as far as the fundamentalist reads, he might indeed have cause to claim that evangelicals are compromising with evil. He might then have proof for his claim that evangelicals are appeasing evil by approving of worldly practices. Fortunately, however, Henry goes on to make it clear that he is *not* approving of these things. He is simply protesting against an implicit legalism that has be-

[4]Carl Henry, *Christian Personal Ethics*, Grand Rapids, Eerdmans, 1957, p. 422.

come predominant in much of the fundamentalist ethics.
As Henry himself puts it, he —

> *. . . is not arguing for drinking, for smoking, for dancing,
> for gambling, even for movie-attendance.* But he is con-
> cerned lest Christians confuse ethical living with an arbi-
> trary legalistic bondage. He is concerned lest externals be-
> come so prominent that internal virtue and vices are not
> treated at all.[5]

Evangelicals have criticized the fundamentalist's over-
emphasis on his code. But they have also made it plain
that what they are arguing against is the legalistic spirit
that threatens the true meaning of the Christian ethic. Thus,
we find it very hard to see any truth in the claim that
evangelicalism is growing on the appeasement of evil.

D. Is Evangelicalism a Movement Doomed by the Judgment of God's Word?

There may be elements of evangelicalism that God is
displeased with,[6] but Ashbrook has failed to show that this
is so. With a great display of unsupported verbosity, he
has anathematized a movement he obviously dislikes. Then,
convinced that God is on his side, he attempts to lend an
aura of divine authority to his anathema by confidently
asserting that evangelicalism "is a movement doomed by the
judgment of God's Holy Word." While there are undoubtedly aspects of evangelicalism that are deserving of
criticism and rebuke, it is obvious that Mr. Ashbrook has
not yet discerned them.

II. ARE EVANGELICALS DIVISIVE?

Richard V. Clearwaters describes what he calls the
"double divisiveness" of the new evangelicalism.

> The New Evangelicalism is doubly divisive: It has divided
> fundamentalists in two groups: fundamentalists and con-
> servatives; and it has divided modernists into two groups:
> modernists and liberals. It has thus made four groups or

---

[5]*Ibid,* p. 426 (italics mine).
[6]We are referring to the fact that men invariably fall short of God's
standard (Rom. 3:23).

classes in the Protestant Christian church and divisively divided these four groups into three divisions.[7]

It seems exceedingly strange to blame evangelicalism for dividing modernism into two groups. After all, if you have one religious group that emphasizes the immanence of God (almost to the point of pantheism) and the inherent goodness of man and another group that stresses the transcendence of God (almost to the point of deism) and speaks of the utter sinfulness of man, these two groups (regardless of how hostile they may both be to orthodoxy) ought to be distinguished in some way.

Clearwaters' other argument, that evangelicals have divided the fundamentalist camp into two groups — fundamentalists and conservatives — raises some interesting questions. Clearwaters himself is a *Conservative* Baptist. Are we then to understand that he is not a fundamentalist? And if Clearwaters is not a fundamentalist, then why is he criticizing evangelicalism? But, of course, Clearwaters *is* a fundamentalist. The point of all this is that these terms are exceedingly ambiguous and one gets the impression that Clearwaters is capitalizing on this vagueness. But more to the point, it is hardly being true to the facts to blame evangelicals for dividing orthodoxy. We have shown in chapter 2 of this book that Henry, Clark and Carnell considered themselves fundamentalists, called themselves fundamentalists and defended fundamentalism during the late 1940's and early 1950's. It was not until fundamentalism began to resist their efforts to awaken the movement to a recognition of its neglected responsibilities that the break between fundamentalism and evangelicalism began.

III. ARE EVANGELICALS UNWILLING TO DEFEND THE FAITH?

This accusation has actually been made by Dr. Ernest Pickering. In his words, evangelicals have shown —

> . . . an unwillingness to continue in a constant, vigorous defense of the faith. New Evangelicals express impatience

[7]Richard V. Clearwaters, "The Double Divisiveness of the New Evangelicalisms," *Central Conservative Baptist Quarterly*, Summer, 1958.

and disdain with those who expose the sin and error of apostasy and long to forget the whole fundamentalist-modernist controversy and move on to something more "constructive." They have grown weary in the battle, and have decided that the advice of the old frontiersman is wise, "If you can't lick 'em, jine 'em."[8]

One is inclined to ask the author of these words where he has been during the last twenty years. And if he has been around, then one must wonder what type of literature he has been reading, for no one who has kept in touch with the publications of orthodox theologians and philosophers could possibly accuse evangelicals of an "unwillingness to continue in a constant, vigorous defense of the faith." With few exceptions, the major orthodox writings in the last two decades in the fields of apologetics and Christian evidences have been produced by men who are evangelicals (or, at least, not fundamentalists). In the general area of apologetics, one can think of Carnell's *Introduction to Christian Apologetics, Philosophy of the Christian Religion,* and *The Kingdom of Love and the Pride of Life,* Clark's *Christian View of Men and Things* and *Religion, Reason and Revelation,* Henry's *Remaking the Modern Mind* and many others. In the area of Christian evidences, Bernard Ramm's *Protestant Christian Evidences* is one of the few works that comes to mind. With regard to the defense of inspiration and propositional revelation, Ramm's *Special Revelation and the Word of God* and Henry's symposium, *Revelation and the Bible,* stand out. These and other evangelical writings constitute most of orthodoxy's *published* defense of the faith. Where, one must ask, is the evangelical's "unwillingness" to defend the faith?

But perhaps Pickering's answer would be, "Yes, these men have written books on apologetics but their so-called 'defense' of Christianity is little more than a capitulation to the positions of liberalism or neo-orthodoxy." It is difficult to conceive of anyone possibly making this claim, but the simplest way to determine its truth or falsity is to examine the literature that these men have produced. Such a study

[8]Ernest Pickering, "The Present Status of the New Evangelicalism," *Central Conservative Baptist Quarterly,* Fall, 1958.

will reveal, we believe, that any search for an evaluation and criticism of these heterodox movements can hardly afford to ignore the contributions of the evangelicals. When the young Christian college or seminary student wants help in evaluating the weaknesses of neo-orthodoxy, for example, where else can he really turn than to the writings of these men[9] whom, we are told, are "unwilling" to defend the faith?

IV. DOES EVANGELICALISM PREACH A POSITIVISM WITHOUT A NEGATIVISM?

Again we find that it is Ernest Pickering who makes this accusation in another issue of *The Conservative Baptist Quarterly*.[10] It may be that in the evangelical's attempt to counter the implicit legalism and hyper-negativism so prevalent in fundamentalist ethics, he has not always expressed all that should be said on the other side. But one can hardly accuse evangelicals of saying nothing about the negative aspect of Christian living. As an example, let us see what Carl Henry has written on the subject.

> As Christian ethics must stand against poor reasons for abstaining from certain practices, it must also stand against bad reasons for indulging in other practices. The Scriptures draw up a rather imposing list of sinful actions and attitudes . . . .
>
> The Pauline list of pagan vices is as conspicuous in his letter as is his tally of Christian virtues . . . here he (Paul) lists a frightening number of sins ranging from adultery and fornication to drunkenness and revelings . . .
>
> The ethical teaching of Jesus excludes as sin much that the Pharisee (and the Christian believer) would be prone to excuse in himself. Not only the act of adultery, but also the lustful look; not only murder, but also the flush of anger come under his condemnation. He also considers as sinful the ambiguous oath, hypocritical religious observances, and pretentious charitable acts.[11]

Since this statement represents the evangelical answer, it is sufficient, we believe, to refute the charge.

[9]We realize that Cornelius Van Til's *New Modernism* and other writings are exceptions. But Van Til is hardly a fundamentalist!
[10]Spring, 1959.
[11]Henry, *Christian Personal Ethics*, op. cit., p. 424f.

V. ARE EVANGELICALS SURRENDERING SOME BASIC CHRISTIAN BELIEFS?

Several have answered this question in the affirmative. John W. Sanderson of Westminster Theological Seminary summarizes[12] the views of other critics by writing that, in its dialogue with liberals, evangelicalism "has adopted some of Liberalism's arguments while at the same time being vague about the verities of the Gospel."[13] Again he writes, "Neo-Evangelicals, so anxious to carry on conversations with Liberals, are in danger of absorbing Liberalism's attitudes, at the cost of losing the sharp edge of Evangelicalism's basic beliefs."[14]

But this charge which is so often made is seldom documented. Which doctrinal belief is in danger of being surrendered? Is it the deity of Christ? or salvation by grace through faith? or the virgin birth of Christ? or the second coming? or is it, perhaps, the inspiration of the Scriptures? While the fundamentalist seeks to advance his cause against evangelicalism with such sweeping generalizations, the discerning Christian wants documentation and facts. Which doctrines are being surrendered and by whom and, most important of all, where is the proof? When faced by these questions, fundamentalists usually take refuge in vague remarks about how the evangelicals are surrendering the orthodox view of the Bible. But again, we say, look at the literature. Where can one find a clearer defense of propositional revelation than in Ramm's *Special Revelation and the Word of God* or a more earnest defense of the inerrancy of the Scriptures than in Clark's *Religion, Reason and Revelation?* We believe that the three chapters of this book devoted to a study of evangelicalism's attitude toward the

[12]Sanderson does not make it clear whether or not he himself concurs with this statement.

[13]John W. Sanderson, "Neo-Evangelicalism and its Critics," *Sunday School Times,* Jan. 28, 1961, p. 74. See also Edward Young, "Where are we Going?" *Presbyterian Guardian,* May-June, 1959.

[14]*Ibid.,* p. 82. See the following articles by Sanderson which are also in the *Sunday School Times:* "Fundamentalism and its Critics," Jan. 21, 1961; "Fundamentalism and Neo-Evangelicalism — Whither?", Feb. 4, 1961; "Purity of Testimony — or Opportunity?", Feb. 11, 1961.

Bible are sufficient reasons for saying that these apprehensions about the evangelical position toward the Bible or any doctrine on which the Christian faith is based are ungrounded.

VI. CONCLUSION

Surely, anything we could say now in conclusion would be, in a sense, anti-climactic. The facts are in and the conclusions are clear. The charges implying that evangelicals are perhaps half-hearted heretics, i.e., men who are beginning to drift away from the basic centralities of the Christian faith, are totally without support. In most cases, we have found that the critics themselves evidence a general unfamiliarity with evangelical literature. It is unfortunate, however, that such crude misrepresentations will continue to gain a hearing in conservative circles and will continue to cloud and confuse the real facts concerning evangelicalism.

CHAPTER 11

Evangelicals: The Misguided Brethren?

CHAPTER 11

Evangelicals: The Misguided Brethren?

Many critics of evangelicalism refuse to go as far as those we have already noticed. They believe that evangelicals are Christian brethren who are sincere, but mistaken about some very important matters.

A recent book written from this perspective is Robert Lightner's *Neo-Evangelicalism*. We believe there are several reasons why its arguments and weaknesses should be considered in this book: (1) There are factors that suggest that it will have an important part in influencing many segments of fundamentalism in their attitude toward evangelicalism, (2) There are a number of misunderstandings and misrepresentations of evangelicalism in the book that suggest that whatever influence it does have among fundamentalists will not help the advancement of truth about this matter. No one can be blamed for wanting to criticize a movement that he thinks is bad. However, it is wrong to attack a movement (even though it might be dangerous) with arguments that are unsupported or false. (3) Our discussion of Lightner's book will give us one final opportunity to notice some more of the basic differences between fundamentalism and evangelicalism. (4) It is of course necessary that the mistaken objections of the book be answered.

I. Turning the Tables

One of the most obvious weaknesses of Lightners' argument is that he is frequently guilty of the same errors he finds so offensive in evangelicalism. For example, he writes,

A perusal of the dissatisfaction of the neo-evangelical leaders (with fundamentalism) will reveal three stupendous (sic) weaknesses. First, they rest on a faulty premise. . . . Secondly, they are too universally condemning. . . . Thirdly, the weaknesses as presented by neo-evangelicals often misrepresent the doctrinal views of fundamentalists.[1]

We believe that Lightner has made it very easy for us to "turn the tables" on him; that is, we shall use Lightner's own objections as examples of the very mistakes he makes. Some might object that our procedure is an *ad hominem* argument, i.e., an argument that attempts to sidestep the force of an objection by diverting attention to other (usually irrelevant) weaknesses in the position of the objector. However, an argument like this is *ad hominem* only when the original objections are ignored or avoided. Since we shall in the course of our remarks deal with his criticisms of evangelicalism, we believe that our procedure will be perfectly valid.

A. Lightner's Arguments Rest on Faulty Premises

First of all, we must see how Lightner believes that the evangelical argument depends on a faulty premise. He is shocked by what he considers to be evangelical statements to the effect that the war between modernism and fundamentalism is over. He attempts to counter this by arguing that there are still modernists around and there are still fundamentalists who are fighting them. One could easily challenge, this writer believes, Lightner's claim that assertions about the war between fundamentalism and modernism being over constitute any major part of the evangelical objection to fundamentalist tactics. But aside from this, it is clear that Lightner's remarks completely miss the point. A careful reading of his argument[2] will reveal that the supposed disagreement between him and the evangelical on this matter is only a verbal dispute. The evangelical would concede that in *Lightner's* sense of the word, modernism (i.e., any kind of unbelief toward the Scriptures or basic

---

[1]Robert Lightner, *Neo-Evangelicalism*, Findlay, Ohio, Dunham Publishing Co. 1962, pp. 42ff.
[2]*Ibid.*, p. 42.

doctrines of the faith) is still around. But in the sense in which evangelicals use the word, modernism (i.e., the "old" liberalism with its belief in the inherent goodness of man and the immanence of God) has, to a great extent, seen its better days.

But what can be said about the premises of Lightner's own argument? For one thing, he simply takes it for granted that fundamentalism as it stands today is the faithful descendant of early fundamentalism. But this is the very point under dispute. Evangelicals are arguing that fundamentalism is no longer what it was fifty years ago. Its accretion of doctrinal and ethical non-essentials and its defaulting of its responsibilities in many areas makes Lightner's equating of the two movements, i.e., the old and the contemporary fundamentalism, very doubtful. It would surprise and perhaps shock many contemporary fundamentalists to realize how many articles contained in the original *Fundamentals* they would disagree with. Lightner hints that the new label of evangelicalism may serve to cover up a new product. But he is just as mistaken when he assumes that the old label (fundamentalism) covers the same product.

B. Lightner's Criticisms of Evangelicalism Are Too General and Universal

It is an interesting comment on the frailties of human nature that Lightner warns others against making this mistake. Too often, he complains, "One man associated with the movement who is an extremist is paraded as representative of the entire movement without any consideration of change or deviation."[3] It is unfortunate that Lightner did not heed his own warning for one of the things he does most frequently is to let one or two men, whose conclusions are not always accepted by other evangelicals, speak for the whole movement. He constantly cites Carnell's position as set forth in his *Case for Orthodox Theology* as representative

[3]*Ibid.*, p. 149.

of what all neo-evangelicals believe.[4] In fact, he even notices that other evangelicals have criticized Carnell[5] without drawing the proper conclusion that Carnell's position is not always representative of evangelicalism as a whole.

In broad sweeping generalizations, Lightner accuses evangelicals of "amalgamation with unbelief" (p. 138), of substituting intellectualism for faith (p. 121) and of doctrinal neglect (p. 119). He states that evangelicals no longer stress the five fundamentals and suggests this as an explanation of their supposed "doctrinal fuzziness" (p. 106).

On page 92, he correctly notes that some Conservative Baptists (particularly a few vocal ones connected with the *Central Conservative Baptist Quarterly*) have criticized evangelicalism. His remarks lend themselves to a mistaken notion that *all* Conservative Baptists are opposed to evangelicalism — something that is far from being the truth! Lightner states confidently that the National Association of Evangelicals represents neo-evangelicalism (p. 75). On the contrary, some of the Arminian denominations within the NAE have little sympathy with the Calvinistic neo-evangelicalism of Clark and Henry. In fact, a great many of the local churches whose denominations belong to the NAE still think of themselves as fundamentalist churches. Apparently not satisfied with these factual blunders, Lightner ventures out into another area — that of eschatology — and makes the remarkable statement that evangelicals are *post-millennialists!* Such assertions as this are clear evidence that fundamentalist critics of evangelicalism are not reading the writings of those they are attacking. However, Lightner's ascription of post-millennial tendencies to evangelicals would probably be a minor point except for the fact that he then proceeds to draw a host of unwarranted conclusions about the evangelical's concern for social progress from their supposed desire to "bring in the kingdom." While Lightner

---

[4]It is significant that Lightner never quotes from any of the many other books Carnell has written. Apparently, he overlooks the possibility of "change, development or deviation" in Carnell's position.
[5]*Ibid.*, p. 109.

insists that his book "is intended to clarify, not camouflage, the new evangelicalism and its dangers,"[6] one must conclude that he has done anything but succeed.

C. Lightner Misrepresents the Doctrines of Evangelicalism

Lightner argues that this is true of evangelicalism's critique of fundamentalism. But of the three examples he offers as proof, two are debatable and rather insignificant points,[7] and the third, namely, the neo-orthodox misrepresentation of the fundamentalist doctrine of inspiration, does not even apply to evangelicalism!

But how faithfully has Lightner represented the doctrines of evangelicalism? We have already noticed his unfortunate remarks about the supposed post-millennialism of evangelicals and his incorrect claim that the National Association of Evangelicals is an organization of evangelicals only. However, he says more. In a very strange chapter, he blames evangelicalism for placing too much emphasis on the doctrine of salvation! One would hardly think this a criticism of a *Christian* movement, especially in the light of the fact that Jesus Himself said that His primary purpose was "to seek and to save that which was lost." Lest anyone doubt that Lightner actually says this, let us notice what he says:

> Without question, both in expression of belief and in practice, the doctrine which is stressed most by the new evangelicalism is the doctrine of salvation. This doctrine with its individual and societal aspects seems to be to neo-evangelicals what the heart is to the human body. It is the vibrant, pulsating and life-giving center of the movement. . . . Could it be possible that the new evangelicalism has put soteriology in the place of the five fundamentals?[8]

But could it be that Lightner and fundamentalism have forgotten that these five fundamentals are, in fact, all

[6]*Ibid.*, p. 8.
[7]Namely, evangelicals assert that fundamentalists believe in the possibility of a pure church (which claim, incidentally, is based on one isolated remark from Carnell) and evangelicals disparage the fundamentalist's lack of social concern. See Lightner, p. 45f.
[8]*Ibid.*, p. 67.

concerned with salvation? The virgin birth, vicarious death and bodily resurrection of Christ were necessary elements in God's provision for salvation; Christ's visible and bodily return to earth is a necessary element in the completion of salvation; and an inspired Bible is a necessary element in the communication of God's plan of salvation. It is indeed strange to see one conservative criticizing another for emphasizing the doctrine of salvation too much! We do not wish to minimize the importance of the five fundamentals, but we remind the reader of our earlier claim that fundamentalists have tended to reduce all of Christian doctrine to these five points. Is this not what Lightner has done?

Furthermore, Lightner contributes to a misrepresentaton of evangelicalism by sometimes quoting from sources that are obviously inaccurate. For example, he quotes L. Harold DeWolfe, a leading representative of contemporary liberalism, as saying that evangelicals "avoid teaching 'verbal' inspiration of the Bible, stressing rather plenary or full inspiration."[9] We have already explained in an earlier chapter how a liberal like DeWolfe could make this mistake. Anyone who begins with a misunderstanding of the orthodox view of inspiration (i.e., who equates "verbal inspiration" with dictation) will naturally regard the "unveiling" (to him) of the actual orthodox doctrine as a change in position.

Another time, Lightner takes note of Reinhold Niebuhr's criticism of Billy Graham because Graham's preaching is too literal and too individualistic. Fundamentalists must indeed be hard-pressed to find objections against evangelicalism if they are forced, like Lightner, to cite liberal criticisms that are equally applicable to their own position.

As if this were not enough, there are even times when Lightner's handling of his quotations is unreliable because he obviously (but unintentionally) twists the original sense of the author. For example, he appeals to Marcius Taber's article, "Fundamentalist Logic," cited earlier in this book. Lightner claims (with Taber as his authority) that liberals

[9]*Ibid.*, p. 132.

"see contradictions and illogic in the new evangelicalism. As a matter of fact, they ridicule the fundamentalist logic as it relates to the inerrancy of the Bible.[10] By *fundamentalist* here they mean new evangelical."[11] Lightner's last remark is not true to Taber's original meaning. In fact, had Lightner read Taber's article more carefully, he would realize that Taber's charges of illogic apply with equal force to his own position as well.

As a final example of Lightner's frequent misrepresentation of evangelicalism, let us consider his remarks about evangelical colleges. He writes,

> In addition to the increased doctrinal concessions there is a considerable rise in the spread of neo-evangelicalism as it is being espoused by many in responsible places of leadership. This is true, especially in educational institutions. . . . (In these schools) the Bible is being de-emphasized (sic). Young men who felt called to the ministry are being encouraged to major in everything else but the Bible.[12]

This kind of talk is not only dangerously misleading, but it is also irresponsible. None of these charges are backed up by facts. Since he himself was trained exclusively in fundamentalist and dispensational schools, he apparently has no personal knowledge of the truth of these remarks. Is Lightner unaware that many of the founders and present leaders of the Accrediting Association of Bible Schools and Bible Colleges are men sympathetic to neo-evangelicalism? Is he unaware (and this is just one point of many that could be scored here) that each school accredited by this association requires a minimum of thirty hours of Bible courses and ten hours of theology? Does this sound like the Bible is being de-emphasized? And of course, we could point out that the true measure of a Christian college is not to be found in the *quantity* of the Bible taught.[13] One of the pri-

10Apparently, Lightner does not realize that he has lent unwitting support to our earlier claim that evangelicals have not surrendered the doctrine of biblical inerrancy!

11*Ibid.*, p. 100.

12*Ibid.*, p. 162.

13Within recent years, a fundamentalist college associated with Mr. Lightner's denomination *reduced* the required number of Bible courses. No cry of protest was then raised about any "de-emphasis" of the Bible. Apparently this is a crime only when the institution in question is evangelical!

mary responsibilities of a Christian college is to integrate all areas of knowledge around the basic concepts of biblical theism. Lightner is grieved that young men called to the ministry are urged to major in non-biblical areas. But has he forgotten that these men have at the same time often been advised to take graduate work in theological seminaries? A seven-year program preparing a man for the ministry provides ample time to major in Bible in seminary. In such cases, an undergraduate Bible major (which would be essential for men not going on to seminary) often produces needless repetition in some courses while keeping the student from a liberal arts background that will make his theological studies more relevant to the needs of the day.

Instead of giving us significant reasons why we should repudiate evangelicalism, Lightner has only shown us something of the same general confusion that pervades most fundamentalist thinking on the subject. But let us continue our study of his work by taking a different approach.

II. THE SAME OLD STORY

Many of Lightner's remarks provide additional support for many of our earlier claims about the weaknesses of fundamentalism. In many ways, he exhibits the same characteristics of fundamentalism that produced the evangelical reaction. We shall notice only three.

A. A Naive Attitude Toward Difficult Questions

Time and again we have noticed how the evangelical does not shirk his responsibility to square his faith with the facts. This does not mean a subordination of Christian essentials to unproven naturalistic assumptions. Oftentimes the fundamentalist continues to cling to theological oddities (like the supposed "gap" between Geness 1:1 and 1:2) and doctrinal non-essentials (like the supposition that man has only been on earth for 6,000 years)[14] only because he seems not to have faced all of the facts. Lightner writes,

[14]We have called the age of man a doctrinal non-essential because the basic problem for Christian theology is *how* man got here (i.e., the origin of man) and not *how long* he has been here.

Another area of vagueness, which will only be touched upon here, is the relation of science to Scripture. How concessive ought the evangelical be to science? Vagueness in this area is further aided by many articles which . . . leave more questions unanswered than are answered. . . . There seems to be an abundance of unnecessary attempts to reconcile the Bible with science.[15]

We could ask, of course, is it unnecessary to reconcile the Bible with science? Is Lightner suggesting that we ignore these problems? Or is he claiming that if we accept *his* interpretation of the scientific data and *his* interpretation of Scripture that the problems will disappear? Many scientists will have difficulties doing the first of these (after all, Lightner is not a trained scientist) and many theologians (even conservatives) will sometimes hesitate to do the second. Perhaps the unanswered questions and the occasionally vague answers to other questions are due to the simple fact that these are exceedingly complicated problems that require us to go slow and not dogmatize.

B. A Dogmatic Attitude Toward Ambiguous Problems

Lightner is dissatisfied with what he considers to be evangelical vagueness in the area of eschatology (the doctrine of last things). He believes that there is too much fluidity in the evangelical position inasmuch as evangelicals deal only with the broad aspects of God's future dealings with man and discuss only such basic determinative issues as the Second Coming of Christ and the coming judgment. Instead, Lightner wishes that they would spend more time dealing with the particular items of prophecy that precede and follow the Second Coming. However, the "vagueness" that Lightner criticizes is not due to any failure of evangelicals to formulate a position.[16] Rather, they recognize that many of these fine points of Bible prophecy are not clearly defined. This partially accounts for the wide differences of opinion about them. Evangelicals would rather emphasize

---

15*Ibid.*, p. 82f.

16We should perhaps point out that Lightner would not be made any more happy even if evangelicals should spell out their views. For with few exceptions, evangelical beliefs would differ widely from Lightner's dispensational pre-tribulationism.

the obvious essentials that all conservatives are agreed upon[17] and not insist that others accept their opinions. Unfortunately, many fundamentalists (including Lightner) think these minor matters should be added to our twentieth-century church creeds. He tell us,

> Flexibility in major areas of eschatology (millennialism, tribulationism and dispensationalism) is both serious and dangerous (sic). It is serious because it produces bewilderment and uncertainty. It is dangerous because eschatology not only relates to the future but to the present as well.[18]

Lightner goes on to add that "these major areas determine the entire course of a theological system. The essential eschatological interpretations . . . lie at the basis of either a literal or allegorical interpretation of Scripture. Eschatological interpretations have a definite bearing upon many of the other doctrines which one holds."[19] This is a claim often made by dispensationalists but its fallacy is exposed when one realizes that the choice between a literal or spiritual interpretation of the Bible is not an either/or situation. By this I mean, no one interprets the Bible *literally or spiritually* all of the time. Of all the factors that one takes into consideration in determining whether a particular passage is literal or spiritual (such as its context, the language used, etc.) the non-dispensationalist usually finds eschatological factors least important. Evidently the dispensationalist feels that our church creeds[20] are inadequate because they do not include pronouncements on such matters as a pretribulation rapture or the identification of the 144,000. Fortunately, most Christians will find these assertions and demands excessive.

[17]However, evangelicals have published much in this area: see Ladd's *Blessed Hope*, Bass' *Backgrounds to Dispensationalism*, Payne's *Imminent Appearing of Christ*, and others.
[18]*Ibid.*, p. 80f.
[19]*Ibid.*, p. 81.
[20]On p. 120, Lightner actually expresses his displeasure that faculty members of a proposed Christian university would only be required to assent to the Apostle's Creed. The fundamentalist dissatisfaction with the historic creeds only supports our contention that fundamentalism has elevated a host of secondary doctrines to a place of undue prominence.

C. An Equivocal Attitude Toward Clear Questions

Much of what we have already said could be repeated here. Again and again, fundamentalist critics like Lightner take matters which evangelical literature has been quite definite about and confuse the issues at stake. As a final example, Lightner states that one of the primary objectives of evangelicalism has been to "present orthodoxy once again in such a way that it will be brought back into the main stream of theological current and again become a live option."[21] In other words, evangelicals want to make orthodoxy more respectable. That evangelicalism has succeeded to some extent in this venture is attested to by many facts — e.g., the success of *Christianity Today*, the testimonies of many non-conservative theologians like William Hordern and Arnold Hearn, and the renewed interest in orthodoxy among previously uncommitted pastors and theological students. However, Lightner claims that evangelicalism has failed to bring orthodoxy back into the main stream of theological thought and as proof, he cites a number of sources antagonistic to evangelicalism. Aside from the fact that he is careful only to quote those sources that support his argument, it is doubtful if his conclusion follows anyway. The neo-evangelical realizes full well that he will never win the leaders of liberalism or neo-orthodoxy to his way of thinking. His objective is the winning of the many experienced pastors and inexperienced theological students who are uncommitted or confused or dissatisfied with their present position. Along with these, of course, he hopes to challenge the unbiblical assumptions of those presently satisfied with their liberalism. It is to be expected that the leaders of liberalism and neo-orthodoxy will resist such efforts and to quote their antagonistic comments hardly constitutes a proof that evangelicalism has failed. In this day of uncertainty, many pastors and Christian workers trained in liberal seminaries are turning from the inadequacies of liberalism to a more biblical theology and, most important of all, to the Christ of the Bible. Many wavering

21*Ibid.*, p. 95.

students are having their faith strengthened as they see an orthodoxy that is able to speak to the needs of the day as well as answer its critics.

III. CONCLUSION

To sum up then, Lightner's criticisms of neo-evangelicalism seem to boil down to this: the evangelical is wrong because he adopts the same methods as Lightner and other fundamentalists; because he emphasizes salvation too much; because he does not dogmatically force his peculiar interpretations of eschatology on others; because he makes the church creeds his test of orthodoxy[22]; because he refuses to over-simplify difficult problems relating to science and the Bible; and finally, because some liberals (of all people) don't like evangelicalism. To some this may seem like an unfair picture of Lightner's arguments, but has he really said any more than this? Many Christians will find that these supposed "weaknesses" of evangelicalism are not defects at all but, in fact, elements of an orthodoxy whose ministry is faithful to Christ, true to God's Word and relevant to the contemporary needs of man.

---

[22]It will not do here to reply that the Bible is the test of orthodoxy, for someone must always decide what it is that the Bible says, and this will be a creed.

Part Six

CONCLUSION

A Warning, a Question, and a Statement of Purpose

We have presented only a *partial* picture of *some* of the trends in *one* of several movements within contemporary Christian orthodoxy. Our discussion has been intentionally limited in scope. In this last chapter, we shall attempt to tie a few loose ends together.

I. A WARNING: THE TEST OF OUR POSTERITY

So far, most of our remarks have been directed to non-evangelicals. The time has come to say a few things to those of our readers who are evangelicals. The history of the Christian Church records that many fine and noble movements began as reactions to excesses or deficiencies in the established church. Lutheranism was a necessary reaction against the superstition, Pelagianism and idolatry of the Roman Catholic Church. The emphasis of Lutheranism on right doctrine was important but, unfortunately, the day came when it had degenerated into a cold, formal orthodoxy that came to be known as "Protestant Scholasticism." The same story has been repeated many times with other reactionary movements such as Pietism, Methodism and, of course, fundamentalism.

We have argued that fundamentalism was a necessary reaction to the unbelief that had settled in the established denominations but it also produced excesses which eventually produced the need for the evangelical reaction about which we have written. With history as our teacher, with human nature as our enemy, and with the Word of God as our judge, it would be strange indeed if evangelicalism did not contain within itself elements that might eventually negate and nullify its effectiveness. Evangelicals must constantly be on their guard against such tendencies.

One of the most obvious and important signs of whether evangelicalism is staying right or straying wrong will be found in its spiritual and academic posterity. What of the students who are being trained by evangelical professors? Do they possess the same degree of spirituality and devotion to Christ as former generations? Is there the same interest in personal evangelism and missionary activity? Today's evangelicals have had the privilege of a strong religious heritage that in spite of its weaknesses has grounded them in the verities of the Christian faith. They must be just as certain to give their students this same confidence in the Word of God. Evangelicals must emphasize love and tolerance but not at the expense of sound doctrine.

Should evangelicalism ever fail to ground its young Christians in what they ought to believe, if it ever begins to lead young Christians into doubt instead of confidence, if it should ever produce a generation of unfaithful or unbelieving Christians, we would then be forced to say that such a movement had forfeited its right to the name of "evangelicalism."

II. A Question: Is Neo-Evangelicalism New?

Do the views discussed in this book deserve to be referred to as "The *New* Evangelicalism"? Undoubtedly, when the term was coined, it had the appeal of novelty and freshness. Unfortunately, many of evangelicalism's present-day woes are due to misunderstandings of the prefix, "neo-." Many Christians, not being familiar with the writings of these men, are concerned over the implications of a *new* evangelicalism. Still others (accidentally or intentionally) confuse it with neo-orthodoxy or the dialectical theology. The slogan that "we don't need any *new* evangelicalism for the *old* one is good enough," has become almost a battle cry for some fundamentalists.

Even though we have made numerous references

throughout this book to the new evangelicalism,[1] it is this writer's firm conviction that the term is a misnomer. It is also dangerous in that it tends to foster confusion and tension among conservatives who do not completely understand it. Furthermore, the name is misleading because many of the positions held by evangelicals are not new at all. Often, they are simply a return to positions held previously by much of orthodox scholarship but which had become obscured or lost during the fundamentalist-modernist controversy.

As just one example out of many that could be offered to support this last claim, let us consider the presuppositionalist approach to apologetics. This is not really a new way to defend the faith. In actuality, presuppositionalism is simply a logical development of principles implicit in the views of St. Augustine, St. Anselm, Calvin and others.

Carl Henry, commenting on this very fact, states that the pagan schools of philosophy that attacked Christianity lacked a starting point for their philosophy. However, the Christian (as exemplified by the approach of Augustine) began with God and did not find it incongruous to derive the world from Him.

> No Christian philosopher saw the profound implications of the Biblical view more clearly at this point than Augustine. Pagan thought simply could not lead one to the Christ and God, because of the darkness of the unregenerate mind. But if one sets out with the revelational framework, if he begins with God, then all is clear. *Credo ut intelligam*, proclaims Augustine, and in this tradition which affirms that man must "believe in order to understand" he is later succeeded by Anselm and the Reformation thinkers, who likewise insist that one must take revelation ground before the philosophic self-consistency of the Christian world-life view is apparent.[2]

Henry goes on to note that the Thomist synthesis was the first major break with the *credo ut intelligam* approach

[1]Our own wishes to avoid the term altogether were suspended in deference to the present way in which this movement is being mentioned. The name may be an unfortunate one, but it has stuck.
[2]Carl Henry, *Remaking the Modern Mind*, Grand Rapids, Eerdmans, 1946, p. 222.

of Augustine and Anselm. In its place Aquinas substituted his *intelligo ut credam,* reason and natural theology being viewed as preparatory to revealed theology and faith. Modern philosophy brought about the disintegration of Thomism until the recent revival of interest in his approach. Thus, a return to the apologetics of Aquinas (or Butler, Paley or even the philosophical theology of F. R. Tennant) is anything but a return to the classical position of Augustine and Calvin, for the latter requires an approach identical to that taken by contemporary presuppositionalists.

Turning to the matter of doctrinal orthodoxy, Harold John Ockenga writes, "Evangelical Theology is synonymous with fundamentalism or orthodoxy. In doctrine the evangelicals and the fundamentalists are one. . . . The evangelicals and the fundamentalists could sign the same creed."[3]

The evangelical believes in the virgin birth of Christ, His deity, vicarious atonement, bodily resurrection and His literal, physical return to earth. Although evangelicals are carrying on an intense and earnest inquiry into the nature of inspiration, they are unquestioning in their allegiance to the Bible as the inscripturated revelation of God.

If theological problems do exist between *some* fundamentalists and other Christians who would prefer to be known as evangelicals, this writer suggests that it is due to the practice by some fundamentalists of illegitimately elevating minor and inconsequential doctrines to levels of undue importance. If evangelicalism does seem "new" to any people, it only proves how far they have drifted away from the moorings of Reformation theology (and the Scriptures) into the dismal morass of dispensationalism. Fortunately, most Christians recognize that it is still the historic creeds of the Church that define orthodoxy and not the writings of, for example, J. N. Darby. We repeat, then, that as far as the historic creeds and essential doctrines of the faith are concerned, evangelicalism and fundamental-

[3]Harold John Ockenga, "Resurgent Evangelical Leadership," *Christianity Today,* Oct. 10, 1960, p. 13.

ism are one. However, problems will continue to arise as long as some fundamentalists continue to define orthodoxy without regard for the basic creedal requirements of the Church.

It is our contention then that evangelicalism is not "new." On the contrary, evangelicalism is a contemporary movement that is rooted deeply in the foundations of historic orthodox Christianity. It is simply and plainly Christian orthodoxy speaking to the theological, social and philosophical needs of the twentieth century.

III. A STATEMENT OF PURPOSE

We shall conclude our study with a review of evangelical goals and objectives as they are outlined by Ockenga.[4]

(1) Evangelicals want to see a revival of Christianity in the midst of a secular world which, because of its loss of contact with God, is facing imminent destruction.

(2) Evangelicals want to win a new respectability for orthodoxy in academic circles. This requires the production of dedicated scholars who will be prepared to defend the faith on the intellectual's own ground.

(3) Evangelicals want to recapture denominational leadership from within the larger denominations rather than completely abandon these denominations to the forces of contemporary liberalism.

(4) Finally, evangelicals want to make Christianity the mainspring in societal reforms that it once was and that it ought to be.

One of the most obvious theological signs of the day is the growing difference of opinion that is threatening to turn orthodoxy into "a house divided against itself." One of the greatest needs of the hour is a rapprochement of the contending factions within orthodoxy. Differences do exist and, without a doubt, mistakes are being made. But evangelicalism as well as fundamentalism wishes to glorify God, magnify His Son and proclaim His Word. It deserves the opportunity to fulfill this task.

[4]*Ibid.*, p. 14.

BIBLIOGRAPHY

Bibliography

Alton, Everest (ed.) *Modern Science and Christian Faith*. Wheaton, Illinois. Van Kampen Press, 1948.

Ashbrook, William A. "The New Evangelicalism — The New Neutralism." *Central Conservative Baptist Quarterly*, Summer, 1959.

Bass, Clarence. *Backgrounds to Dispensationalism*. Grand Rapids. Eerdmans (c. 1960).

Beck, Lewis White. *Philosophic Inquiry*. Englewood Cliffs, N.Y. Prentice-Hall, Inc. (1959).

Bouma, Clarence. "Orthodox Theological Scholarship." *Calvin Forum*. February, 1950, p. 134.

Buswell, J. Oliver. *Christian View of Being and Knowing*. Grand Rapids. Zondervan (c. 1960).

Bromily, G. W. "The Authority of the Bible: The Attitude of Modern Theologians." *Evangelical Quarterly*. vol. 19. 1947. pp. 127-136. "Church Doctrine of Inspiration," *Revelation and the Bible*, Grand Rapids, Baker Book House (c. 1958).

Carnell, E. J. *Case for Orthodox Theology*. Philadelphia. Westminster Press. 1959.
Christian Commitment. New York. MacMillan. 1957.
"Fundamentalism" in *Handbook of Christian Theology*. (Halvorson, Marvin, ed.) New York. 1958.
Introduction to Christian Apologetics. Grand Rapids. Eerdmans. 1948.
Kingdom of Love and the Pride of Life. Grand Rapids. Eerdmans. 1961.
"Niebuhr's Criterian of Verification" in *Reinhold Niebuhr, His Religious, Social and Political Thought* (ed. by C. W. Kegley and R. W. Bretall) N.Y. 1956.
"Orthodoxy: Cultic vs. Classical." *Christian Century*. March 30, 1960. pp. 377-379.

Philosophy of the Christian Religion. Grand Rapids. Eerdmans. 1952.
"Post-Fundamentalist Faith." *Christian Century*. August 26, 1958. p. 971.
"The Problem of Religious Authority." *His*. February, 1950. pp. 6ff.
The Theology of Reinhold Niebuhr. Grand Rapids. Eerdmans. 1951.

Clark, Gordon H. "Apologetics." *Contemporary Evangelical Thought*. (ed. by Henry) N.Y. Channel Press. 1957.
Christian Philosophy of Education. Grand Rapids. Eerdmans. (c. 1946).
Christian View of Men and Things. Grand Rapids. Eerdmans. 1952.
Religion, Reason and Revelation. Philadelphia. Presbyterian Reformed Publishing Co. 1960.
Thales to Dewey. Boston. Houghton-Mifflin Co. (c. 1957).
"The Bible As Truth." *Bibliotheca Sacra*. April, 1957. pp. 157-170.

Clearwaters, Richard V. "The Double Divisiveness of the New Evangelicalism," *Conservative Baptist Quarterly*, Summer, 1959.

Cole, Stewart G. *History of Fundamentalism*. N.Y. Harper and Bros. 1931.

Curtis, Richard K. "Language and Theory: Some Basic Considerations." *Gordon Review*. Sept., 1955. Dec., 1956. Jan., 1957.

Curtis, Richard K. "The New Evangelicalism." (unpublished paper). Bethel College and Seminary, St. Paul, Minn.

Feinberg, Charles L. (ed.). *The Fundamentals for Today*. Grand Rapids. Kregel Publications. 1958. 2 volumes.

Ferré, Frederick, *Language, Logic and God.* New York. Harper and Bros. (c. 1961).

Ferm, Robert O. *Cooperative Evangelism.* Grand Rapids. Zondervan. (c. 1958).

Furniss, Norman F. *The Fundamentalist Controversy.* New Haven, Conn. Yale University Press. 1954.

Grounds, Vernon. "Fundamentalism Needs a Reformation." *Eternity.* Dec. 1961, pp. 21-29.

"The Nature of Evangelicalism." *Eternity.* Feb., 1956. pp. 12f.

"The Old Biblicism and the New." (unpublished paper) Conservative Baptist Seminary, Denver, Colorado.

"Fundamentalism and Evangelicalism: Legitimate Labels or Illicit Labels?" (unpublished paper). Conservative Baptist Seminary, Denver, Colorado.

Hackett, Stuart C. *Resurrection of Theism.* Chicago. Moody Press. (c. 1957).

Harrison, Everett F. "Criteria of Biblical Inerrancy." *Christianity Today.* Jan. 20, 1958. pp. 14-18.

"The Phenomena of Scripture." *Revelation and the Bible.* (ed. by Henry) Grand Rapids. Baker Book House (c. 1958).

Hearn, Arnold W. "Fundamentalist Renascence." *Christian Century.* April 30, 1958. pp. 528f.

Henry, Carl F. H. *Christian Personal Ethics.* Grand Rapids. Eerdmans. 1957.

(ed.) *Contemporary Evangelical Thought.* Great Neck, N.Y. Channel Press. 1957.

"Dare We Renew the Controversy?" *Christianity Today.* June 24, 1957. pp. 23ff.

"Divine Revelation and the Bible." *Inspiration and Interpretation* (ed. by John Walvoord) Grand Rapids. Eerdmans (c. 1957).

Drift of Western Thought. Grand Rapids. Eerdmans. 1951.

Evangelical Responsibility in Contemporary Theology. Grand Rapids. Eerdmans (c. 1957).

Fifty Years of Protestant Theology. Boston. Wilde (c. 1950).

Giving a Reason for Our Hope. Boston. Wilde (c. 1949).

"Man's Dilemma: Sin" in *The World for This Century* (ed. by M. C. Tenney). N.Y. Oxford. 1949. pp. 3-20.

Notes on the Doctrine of God. Boston. Wilde (c. 1948).

"Perils of Ecumenicity." *Christianity Today.* Nov. 26, 1956. pp. 20-22.

"Perils of Independency." *Christianity Today.* Nov. 12, 1956. pp. 20-23.

Protestant Dilemma. Grand Rapids. Eerdmans. 1949.

Remaking the Modern Mind. Grand Rapids. Eerdmans. (c. 1946).

(ed.) *Revelation and the Bible.* Grand Rapids. Baker Book House. 1958.

The Uneasy Conscience of Modern Fundamentalism. Grand Rapids. Eerdmans. 1947.

"What is this Fundamentalism?" *United Evangelical Action.* July 15, 1956. pp. 303-306.

Hordern, William. *Case for a New Reformation Theology.* Philadelphia. Westminster Press. 1959.

"Is Evangelical Theology Changing?" *Christian Life.* March, 1956. pp. 16ff.

Kantzer, Kenneth. "The Authority of the Bible." *The Word for This Century.* N.Y. Oxford. 1960.

Kik, J. Marcellus. *Ecumenism and the Evangelical.* Philadelphia. Presbyterian and Reformed. 1958.

Kuhn, Harold B. "Philosophy of Religion" in *Contemporary Evangelical Thought.* Great Neck. N.Y. Channel Press. 1957.

Jellema, Dirk. "Ethics." *Contemporary Evangelical Thought.* Ibid.

Jewett, Paul K. "Biblical Authority, a crucial Issue in Protestantism." *United Evangelical Action.* May 1, 1953. p. 3.

"Emil Brunner and the Bible." *Christianity Today.* Jan. 21, 1957. pp. 7-9.

Lightner, Robert. *Neo-Evangelicalism.* Findlay, Ohio. Dunham Publishing Co. 1962.

Machen, J. Gresham. *Christianity*

and Liberalism. Grand Rapids. Eerdmans. 1923.

What Is Christianity? Grand Rapids. Eerdmans. 1952.

McCullough, Paul E. "Shall we Surrender the Term Fundamentalism?" *Baptist Bulletin.* Feb., 1958. pp. 10ff.

McIntyre, Carl. "The New Evangelicalism." *Christian Beacon.* Jan. 9, 1958.

Mixter, Russel L. (ed.) *Evolution and Christian Thought Today.* Grand Rapids. Eerdmans. 1959.

Nash, Ronald H. *Dooyeweerd and the Amsterdam Philosophy.* Grand Rapids. Zondervan. 1962.

"Where Are Our Evangelical Graduate Schools?" *United Evangelical Action.* June, 1961 p. 9f.

Ockenga, Harold John "The New Evangelicalism." *The Park Street Spire.* Feb., 1958.

"Resurgent Evangelical Leadership." *Christianity Today.* Oct. 10, 1960. pp. 11-15.

Orr, James. *Christian View of God and the World.* N.Y. Scribners. (1897).

Inspiration and Revelation. Grand Rapids. Eerdmans. 1952.

"Science and Christian Faith." *The Fundamentals.* Chicago. Testimony Publishing House. vol. 4. pp. 91-104.

Packer, J. I. *Fundamentalism and the Word of God.* Grand Rapids. Eerdmans. 1959.

Pickering, Ernest. "The Present Status of the New Evangelicalism." *Central Conservative Baptist Quarterly.* Fall, 1958 and Spring, 1959.

Pike, Kenneth. "Language and Meaning: Strange Dimension of Truth." *Christianity Today.* May 8, 1961. pp. 690-692.

Ramm, Bernard. "Authority and Scripture: II." *Christian Century.* March 1, 1961. pp. 265-267.

Christian View of Science and Scripture. Grand Rapids. Eerdmans. 1955,

"Evidence of Prophecy and Miracle" in *Revelation and the Bible.* Grand Rapids. Baker. 1958. pp. 251-264.

Pattern of Authority. Grand Rapids. Eerdmans. 1957.

Problems in Christian Apologetics. Portland. Western Baptist Theological Seminary. 1949.

Protestant Biblical Interpretation. Boston. Wilde. 1950.

Protestant Christian Evidences. Chicago. 1953.

Special Revelation and the Word of God. Grand Rapids. Eerdmans. 1961.

Types of Apologetic Systems. Wheaton, Ill. Van Kampen Press. (c. 1953).

The Witness of the Spirit. Grand Rapids. Eerdmans. 1960.

Reid, W. Stanford. "Modernism — Romanism — Fundamentalism — Calvinism." *Calvin Forum.* Dec., 1948. pp. 86-89.

Rushdoony, Rousas. *By What Standard?* Philadelphia. Presbyterian and Reformed. 1959.

Sanderson, John W. "Neo-Evangelicalism and its Critics." *Sunday School Times.* Jan. 28, 1961. p. 74ff.

"Fundamentalism and Its Critics." *Sunday School Times.* Jan. 21, 1961. pp. 58ff.

"Fundamentalism and Neo-Evangelicalism — Whither?" *Sunday School Times.* Feb. 4, 1961. pp. 90ff.

"Purity of Testimony — or Opportunity?" *Sunday School Times.* Feb. 11, 1961.

Thomas, J. T. "The Authority of the Bible." *Theology Today.* July, 1946. pp. 159-171.

Taber, Marcius. "Fundamentalist Logic." *Christian Century.* July 3, 1957. pp. 817f.

Tozer, A. W. "Can Fundamentalism be Saved?" *Christian Life.* August, 1954. pp. 14ff.

Van Til, Cornelius. *Defense of the Faith.* Philadelphia. Presbyterian and Reformed Publishing Co. 1955.

Young, Warren. *A Christian Approach to Philosophy.* Grand Rapids. Baker (c. 1954).

Young, Warren. "Whither Evangelicalism." *Bulletin of the Evangelical Theological Society.* Winter. 1959.

INDEX

Index

187

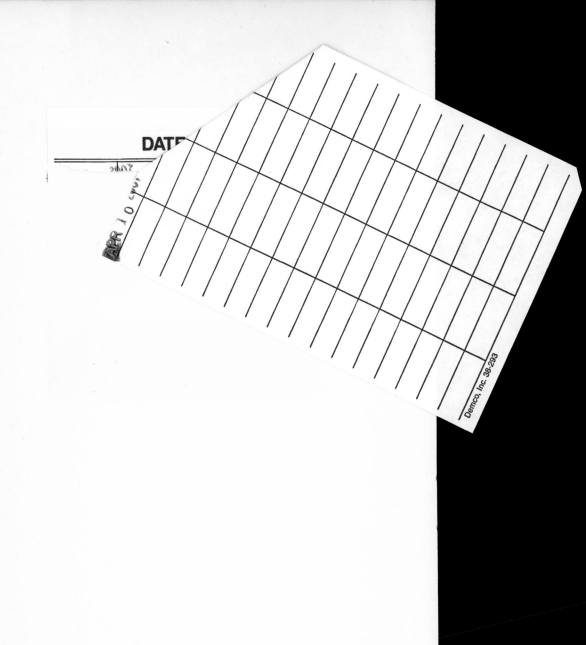